THE
ESSENTIAL
JESUS

The Essential Jesus
© Matthias Media 2008
(St Matthias Press Ltd ACN 067 558 365)

Matthias Media (Australia)
Telephone: (02) 9663 1478; international: +61-2-9663-1478
Email: info@matthiasmedia.com.au
Internet: www.matthiasmedia.com.au

Matthias Media (USA)
Telephone: 330 953 1702; international: +1-330-953-1702
Email: sales@matthiasmedia.com
Internet: www.matthiasmedia.com

The translation of Luke's Gospel used in this book was first produced by
Tony Payne, John Dickson, Greg Clarke and Kirsten Birkett in 2001. It was
reviewed and revised in 2008 by Tony Payne, Peter Bolt, Darrell Bock, Evonne
Paddison, Tim Thornborough and Anne Woodcock.

ISBN 978 1 921441 27 1

Cover design and typesetting by Lankshear Design Pty Ltd.

Welcome to the story of the most extraordinary and influential man ever to have walked on this planet—Jesus of Nazareth.

The biography or 'Gospel' of Jesus' life that you are about to read was written nearly 2000 years ago by a doctor named Luke. It's been speaking to people of every background, race and situation ever since.

Reading the Gospel of Jesus is an opportunity to get back to the real Jesus, *the essential Jesus*, and to discover something new about yourself, about your world and about God.

Previously in the Bible ...

THE GOSPEL OF LUKE IS A BIT LIKE AN EPISODE IN A MAJOR TV series. If this is the first episode you've ever seen, some background is almost essential. So to help you understand what's happening in the Gospel of Luke, who some of the characters are, and where we're up to in the story, here are four brief snapshots from 'previously in the Bible ...'

1. God creates the world

The Bible begins at the very beginning, with God creating the world and everything in it. Three very important pieces of background information flow out of this for reading Luke's Gospel:

- The 'God' who keeps being mentioned in Luke is the God who rules the world. He made the world, and so he's in charge of it. He's the boss, the ruler, the king.
- Unlike most human rulers, God is loving and good. This is seen in the extraordinary and beautiful world that he made. In fact, in the very first chapter of the Bible, God himself describes the world he has just created as being "very good".
- God also made humanity, and put us in charge of the world. Our job is to care for the world and supervise it, under God's authority.

This snapshot from the opening chapters of Genesis (the first book of the Bible) paints a very appealing picture. It's like a perfect kingdom: God is the good and gracious king, and we are his loyal subjects, living in and enjoying the world God has made. It's like those opening scenes in a drama where everything is sunlight and trees and happy families playing on the lawn. You just know that something is about to go wrong.

2. Humanity rebels

A tragedy occurs early in the Bible's story that affects everything that follows. Not content with the good world that God has made and their high position in it, the first humans (Adam and Eve) rebel against God and his rule. They foolishly think that God might be holding out on them and denying them some of what is rightly theirs. So they take matters into their own hands, and defy God's authority and his instructions. God's kingdom is split apart.

This human rebellion becomes one of the key themes in the rest of the Bible. (The Bible often uses the word 'sin' to describe this attitude of rebellion against God.)

3. God the just Judge

The picture we get of God in the Bible is of the best kind of king and ruler—one who loves his people enough to take their rebellion seriously, and to call them to account for their actions. When Adam and Eve disobey God, and reject his rule over them, they suffer the consequences. God judges them and gives them what they ask for. He ejects them from his presence, and lets them discover what life without him is like. But since God is the creator and source of all goodness and life, being cut off from him means disappointment, frustration and death—words that still describe our world today.

So what will happen? Is it the end of God's kingdom? Will God just leave it at that?

4. The cliffhanger

Most of the first half of the Bible (the Old Testament) is taken up with the beginnings of God's plan to rescue humanity and re-establish his kingdom.

God chooses one man (Abraham), and through him a nation (Israel) to be his own special people. Through Israel, God promises to put the world right, and bring humanity back to himself.

However, not everything goes smoothly. Just like Adam and Eve, the Israelites end up rebelling against God. And they also suffer his judgement. So instead of continuing to live in the 'Promised Land' that God had given them, they are invaded, defeated and taken away to live in a foreign country.

The first half of the Bible finishes with a cliffhanger. God's rescue plan seems to be hanging by a thread, but there is hope.

The prophets of Israel had foretold the coming of a new king or 'Christ' who would re-establish the kingdom of God ('Christ' means 'anointed one' or 'king'). He would judge and destroy God's enemies, but bring rescue and salvation for his people. They would no longer be rebels, but loyal and loving subjects of the king.

THESE FOUR SNAPSHOTS FROM 'PREVIOUSLY IN THE BIBLE' give us an idea of what would have been in the minds of the original readers of Luke's Gospel. They were waiting for God to re-establish his kingdom. But as the Gospel of Luke opens, it is around the beginning of the first century AD—some 400 years since the last of these prophecies of hope. The Israelites are back and living in their land, but it is not 'theirs'. They are ruled and occupied by the Romans, and their 'king' (Herod) is a puppet of the Roman authorities.

Now read on …

The Gospel of Jesus, according to Luke

CHAPTER 1[a]

Many have attempted to put together an account of the things that have been fulfilled among us, just as these things were passed on to us by those who from the beginning were eyewitnesses and servants of the message. For this reason, it seemed good to me as well, having investigated everything thoroughly from the start, to write something orderly for you, Most Honourable Theophilus.[b] My aim is that you may know the certainty of the message you were taught.

In the time of Herod, King of Judea,[c] there was a priest called Zechariah from the priestly division of Abijah. He had a wife, Elizabeth, who was descended from the line of Aaron. They were both righteous people before God, living blamelessly according to all the commands and regulations of the Lord. Yet they had no children, because Elizabeth was infertile; and they were both elderly.

Now it happened that Zechariah's division was rostered to perform the priestly duties before God. And according to the custom of the priesthood, he was chosen by lot to go into the

a Luke's Gospel was originally written in Greek, and contained no chapter divisions. These have been added for ease of reading and reference.
b Many ancient pieces of literature were dedicated to important individuals, often the sponsor of the work.
c Herod the Great ruled Jewish Palestine under the authority of the Romans from 37 BC to 4 BC.

temple of the Lord to burn incense. A large crowd outside the temple was praying at the time the incense was burned.

An angel[d] of the Lord appeared to him, standing at the right of the incense altar, and when he saw this, Zechariah was very troubled and afraid.

The angel said to him, "Do not be afraid, Zechariah, because your prayers have been heard—your wife Elizabeth will bear you a son, and you are to give him the name John. He will be a joy and a delight to you, and many will rejoice because of his birth, for he will be great before the Lord. He must not drink wine or strong drink, and he will be filled with the Holy Spirit, even from his mother's womb. He will turn many of the children of Israel back to the Lord their God, and he will go before the Lord in the spirit and power of Elijah,[e] to turn the hearts of fathers to their children, and to turn the disobedient to the wisdom of the righteous. He will prepare a people who are ready for the Lord."

Zechariah said to the angel, "How will I know this is true? For I am an old man and my wife is advanced in age."

The angel replied, "I am Gabriel, who stands in the presence of God. I was sent to speak to you, and make this important announcement to you. But you will be silent and not able to speak until the day these things come about, because you did not believe my message, which will be fulfilled in due course."

In the meantime, the people were waiting for Zechariah, and wondered why he was taking so long in the temple. When he came out, he was unable to speak to them, and they realised that he had seen a vision in the temple. He kept making signs to them, and remained mute.

When the time of Zechariah's service came to an end, he went home. After this, Elizabeth his wife became pregnant. She kept herself out of public view for five months, saying, "So this is how the Lord has acted for me, when he looked kindly on me, and took away my disgrace among the people".

---

d The word 'angel' means 'messenger'.

e Elijah was one of the most famous prophets of the Old Testament, who challenged wayward Israel to come back to God. In one of the prophecies of the Old Testament, it was foretold that Elijah would one day return to Israel to prepare the way for the coming of the Lord.

In the sixth month, the angel Gabriel was sent from God to a city in Galilee[f] called Nazareth, to a virgin who was engaged to a man named Joseph. Joseph was from the family line of David,[g] and the virgin's name was Mary. The angel went to her and said, "Greetings, highly favoured one,[h] the Lord is with you".

But when she heard this, Mary was deeply disturbed, and wondered what sort of greeting this could be.

The angel said to her, "Do not be afraid, Mary, for you have found favour with God. You will become pregnant, and give birth to a son, and you are to call him Jesus. He will be great, and will be called 'Son of the Most High', and the Lord God will give him the throne of his father David. He will rule over the house of Jacob[i] forever, and his kingdom will never end."

Mary said to the angel, "How can this be, since I am a virgin?"

The angel replied, "The Holy Spirit[j] will come upon you, and the power of the Most High will overshadow you. Therefore the child to be born will be holy, and will be called the Son of God. Look, even your cousin Elizabeth has conceived a son in her old age, and is in her sixth month—she who was said to be infertile. So nothing is impossible for God."

Mary said, "I am the Lord's servant. May it all happen to me just as you have said." And the angel left her.

Soon after, Mary got ready and hurried to the hill country, to a city in Judah. She entered Zechariah's home, and called out a greeting to Elizabeth.

When Elizabeth heard Mary's greeting, the baby kicked in her womb, and Elizabeth was filled with the Holy Spirit. She declared in a loud voice, "You are blessed among women, and blessed is the fruit of your womb! And who am I that the mother of my Lord should visit me? For as the sound of your greeting reached my ears, the baby inside my womb kicked with joy. Blessed is she who believed that what the Lord said to her would be fulfilled."

f   A region in northern Israel around Lake Galilee.

g   Israel's greatest king.

h   Literally, 'O one who has received a gracious gift'.

i   'House of Jacob' is another way of saying 'the family or nation of Israel'.

j   That is, God's own Spirit.

And Mary said:

"My soul greatly honours the Lord,
and my spirit rejoices because of God my Saviour,
for he has taken notice of the humble state of his servant.
For from now on, every generation will call me blessed
because the Mighty One has done great things for me—
holy is his name,
and to generation after generation of people, he shows mercy
to those who fear him.
He has shown the strength of his arm, and scattered those
who are arrogant in their hearts;
he has knocked down rulers from their thrones; and he has
lifted up the humble.
He has filled the hungry with good things; but the rich he has
sent away empty.
He has taken care of Israel, his son, remembering to be merciful,
just as he promised to our ancestors, to Abraham[k] and his
descendants for ever."

Mary remained with her for about three months, and then returned home.

Now the time finally came for Elizabeth to have her baby, and she gave birth to a son. Her neighbours and relatives heard that the Lord had shown her great mercy, and they shared her joy.

On the eighth day, they came to have the boy circumcised, and they were going to name him after his father, Zechariah. But his mother said, "No, he is to be called John".

They said to her, "No-one from your family has that name". And they communicated with his father by signs, to see what he wanted to call him.

Zechariah asked for something to write on, and wrote, "His name is John". And they were all amazed.

Immediately, Zechariah's mouth was opened, and his tongue set free, and he began to praise God. And those who lived nearby were filled with awe, and in the Judean mountain region there

k   The ancestor of all the Israelites, the grandfather of Jacob (who was later renamed 'Israel').

was much discussion about all these events. Everyone who heard about it could not help wondering, "What then will this child turn out to be?" For the hand of the Lord was with him.

And his father Zechariah was filled with the Holy Spirit and prophesied:

"Blessed be the Lord God of Israel, because he has visited and redeemed his people;
he has raised up a mighty Saviour[l] for us in the family line of his servant, David,
just as he spoke through his holy prophets of old—
rescue[l] from our enemies and from the hand of all who hate us,
to show the mercy promised to our ancestors and to remember his holy covenant,[m]
an oath which he swore to our father Abraham—to grant us deliverance from the hand of our enemies, that we might serve him all our days without fear
in holiness and righteousness in his presence.
And you, my child, will be called a prophet of the Most High;
for you will go before the Lord, to prepare his way,
to make salvation[l] known to his people by the forgiveness of their sins,
through the compassionate mercy of our God, which will visit us like a sunrise from on high,
to give light to those who sit in darkness and the shadow of death,
to guide our feet into the way of peace."

The boy grew and became strong in spirit; and he lived in the desert until the time when he appeared publicly to Israel.

CHAPTER 2

In those days, a decree went out from Caesar Augustus to conduct a census of the Roman world—this was the first census that took place when Quirinius was governor of Syria. So everyone

---

l 'Rescue/rescuer' and 'salvation/saviour' mean the same thing.

m A covenant is a binding promise, usually with obligations and responsibilities attached. In this case, it refers to the covenant God made with Abraham.

travelled back to their original home towns to register, including Joseph. He went up from Nazareth in Galilee to the city of David (which is called Bethlehem) in Judea,[a] because he was from David's family line. He took Mary his fiancée with him to be registered, and she was pregnant.

And while they were there in Bethlehem, the time came for her to have the baby, and she gave birth to her firstborn son. And because there was no room for them in the inn, she wrapped him in strips of cloth, and used an animal food trough[b] for his cradle.

In that part of the country, there were shepherds who stayed out in the fields at night to keep guard over their flock. Without warning, one of the Lord's angels appeared to them, and the blinding brilliance of the Lord shone all around them. They were terrified, but the angel said to them, "Do not be afraid. Listen, I am here to bring you news of great joy, which is for all the people: today, a Saviour has been born to you in the city of David. He is Christ the Lord. And this will be the sign for you—you will find a child wrapped up in strips of cloth and lying in a food trough."

Suddenly, there appeared with the angel a vast company of the heavenly armies, praising God and saying, "Glory to God in the highest, and peace on earth among those with whom he is pleased".

After the angels had left them and gone back to heaven, the shepherds said to each other, "Come on, let's go into Bethlehem and see this thing that has taken place, which the Lord has made known to us". They went quickly, and discovered Mary and Joseph—and the baby lying in a food trough. When they saw this, they revealed the message that had been told to them about this child, and everyone who heard it was amazed at what the shepherds said. Mary treasured all these things, and thought them over in her heart. The shepherds went back, glorifying and praising God for everything they had heard and seen, which had happened just as they had been told.

After eight days, the time came for him to be circumcised, and they named him Jesus, which was what the angel had said to call him before he was conceived in the womb. And when the

a In the southern region of Israel, close to Jerusalem.
b Traditionally, 'manger'.

THE ESSENTIAL JESUS

days of their purification were over (according to the Law of Moses[c]), Joseph and Mary took him up to Jerusalem to present him to the Lord, just as it is written in the Law of the Lord, "Every firstborn male shall be called holy to the Lord". They also went in order to offer a sacrifice, as the Law of the Lord says: a pair of turtledoves or two young pigeons.

Now there was a man in Jerusalem named Simeon. He was a righteous and devout man, who was waiting for Israel to be comforted; and the Holy Spirit was upon him. It had been revealed to him by the Holy Spirit that he would not see death before he had seen the Lord's Christ.[d]

Through the influence of the Spirit, he went into the temple. And when the parents brought the child Jesus in to do for him what the custom of the law required, Simeon took him in his arms and blessed God, and said,

"Now, Master, you are letting your servant depart in peace, as you promised in your word,
because with my own eyes I have seen your salvation
which you have prepared for all peoples to see—
a light bringing revelation for the nations, and honour for your people Israel."

Jesus' father and mother were amazed at what was said about him, and Simeon blessed them and said to Mary, his mother, "This one is destined to cause the falling and rising of many in Israel, and to be a sign that is spoken against—so the thoughts of many hearts will be revealed (and as for you, a sword will pierce through your own soul)".

In the temple there was also a prophetess called Anna, the daughter of Phanuel, from the tribe of Asher. She was very old, having lived with her husband seven years after her marriage, and then as a widow for eighty-four years. She never left the temple, worshipping God with fasting and prayers night and day.

c Moses was perhaps the most famous leader of Israel in the Old Testament. Moses led Israel out of slavery in Egypt, and it was through Moses that God revealed the laws that he wanted Israel to live by. One of these laws was that all Jewish males had to be circumcised.

d The Christ (sometimes translated 'Messiah') was God's specially anointed, chosen king whom the Jews were waiting for to rescue them from their enemies. He was promised in the Old Testament.

She came up to them at that very moment, and gave thanks to God, and began to speak about the child to all those who were waiting for the redemption of Jerusalem.

When they had finished all that the Law of the Lord required, Joseph and Mary returned to their own city of Nazareth in Galilee. The boy grew and became strong and full of wisdom. And the grace of God was with him.

Each year his parents went to Jerusalem for the Feast of the Passover,[e] and when he was twelve they went up for the Feast according to the custom.

When the days of the Feast were finished, they began their return journey, but the boy Jesus remained behind in Jerusalem without his parents knowing. They thought that he was somewhere in their group, and they had gone a day's journey before they started to look for him among their relatives and friends. Finding nothing, they returned to Jerusalem to search for him. After three days, they found him in the temple, sitting among the teachers, listening to them and asking questions. All those who heard him were astonished at his level of understanding, and his answers.

When they saw him there, his parents were astonished and his mother said to him, "Son, why did you treat us like this? Look, your father and I have been anxiously searching for you."

He said to them, "Why did you have to search for me? Didn't you realise that I must be in my Father's house?" But they didn't understand what he was saying to them.

Then Jesus went back with his parents to Nazareth, and was obedient to them. And his mother treasured all these things in her heart. Jesus grew in wisdom and stature, and in the favour of God and of those who knew him.

CHAPTER 3

It was the fifteenth year of the reign of Tiberius Caesar. Pontius Pilate was governor of Judea, Herod was tetrarch of Galilee, his

---

e One of the great festivals of the Jewish year, on which the Jews remember and celebrate their escape (or Exodus) from slavery in Egypt.

brother Philip tetrarch of Iturea and Traconitis, and Lysanias was tetrarch of Abilene.[a] It was at this time, during the high priesthood of Annas and Caiaphas, that the word of God came to John, the son of Zechariah, in the desert.

He went throughout the country around the Jordan, proclaiming a baptism[b] of repentance[c] for the forgiveness of sins. As it is written in the scroll of the words of Isaiah the prophet:

> "A voice crying out in the desert:
>   'Prepare the way of the Lord;
>   make his paths straight;
>   every valley will be filled in,
>   and every mountain and hill will be levelled;
>   the crooked roads will become straight,
>   and the rough tracks smooth.
>   And all humanity will see the salvation of God.'"

So John said to the crowds that had come out to be baptised by him, "You snakes! Who warned you to flee from the coming wrath?[d] Therefore, produce fruits that are worthy of repentance. And do not start to say to yourselves, 'We have Abraham as our father'. For I tell you that God is able to raise up children of Abraham from these rocks. Indeed, the axe is already poised at the root of the trees; and every tree that does not produce good fruit is cut down and thrown into the fire."

"What should we do then?" the crowds asked him.

He answered them, "The one who has two shirts should donate one to someone who has none; and the one who has food should do the same".

Tax collectors[e] also came to be baptised by him, and said to him, "Teacher, what should we do?"

---

a A tetrarch was the ruler of a smaller region. The Herod and Philip mentioned here were sons of Herod the Great (referred to in Luke chapter 1).

b To baptise something is to plunge or immerse it, usually in water. Being baptised in water was a common Jewish way to indicate that you were making a fresh start.

c Literally, 'a change of outlook or mind', used here of returning to God.

d Or 'anger'; a reference to the day of judgement.

e That is, Jews who collaborated with the occupying Roman forces to collect taxes from their fellow Jews. They were widely hated, and excluded from Jewish religious life.

And John answered them, "Take no more than you are supposed to collect".

Soldiers also asked him, "What about us; what should we do?"

And he said to them, "Don't threaten people for money, or be corrupt, but be content with your wages".

The expectations of the people began to rise, and everyone wondered in their hearts whether he might be the Christ.

In answer to this, John said to all of them, "I baptise you with water; but someone much stronger than me is coming—I would not even be worthy to undo the strap of his sandal. He will baptise you with the Holy Spirit and fire. He has a winnowing fork in his hand to clean out his threshing floor, and gather the wheat into his barn. But he will burn up the chaff with unquenchable fire."[f]

Thus, with many other warnings, John announced the news to the people.

But when John rebuked Herod the tetrarch for taking Herodias, his brother's wife, and for all the other wicked things he had done, Herod added this to them all: he locked up John in prison.

Now when all the people had been baptised, and Jesus also had been baptised and was praying, heaven was opened, and the Holy Spirit came down upon him in bodily form like a dove. And a voice came from heaven, "You are my beloved son; with you I am very pleased".

Jesus himself was about thirty when it all really began. He was the son (so it was thought) of Joseph, who was the son of Heli, the son of Matthat, the son of Levi, the son of Melchi, the son of Jannai, the son of Joseph, the son of Mattathias, the son of Amos, the son of Nahum, the son of Esli, the son of Naggai, the son of Maath, the son of Mattathias, the son of Semein, the son of Josech, the son of Joda, the son of Joanan, the son of Rhesa, the son of Zerubbabel, the son of Shealtiel, the son of Neri, the son of Melchi, the son of Addi, the son of Cosam, the son of

f The threshing floor was an open area about 15 metres in diameter where farmers would take their harvest of grain. To separate the kernels of grain from the chaff (that is, bits of straw and other material), they would shovel the grain into the air using a winnowing fork, allowing the chaff to be blown away by the breeze.

Elmadam, the son of Er, the son of Joshua, the son of Eliezer, the son of Jorim, the son of Matthat, the son of Levi, the son of Simeon, the son of Judah, the son of Joseph, the son of Jonam, the son of Eliakim, the son of Melea, the son of Menna, the son of Mattatha, the son of Nathan, the son of David, the son of Jesse, the son of Obed, the son of Boaz, the son of Sala, the son of Nahshon, the son of Amminadab, the son of Admin, the son of Arni, the son of Hezron, the son of Perez, the son of Judah, the son of Jacob, the son of Isaac, the son of Abraham, the son of Terah, the son of Nahor, the son of Serug, the son of Reu, the son of Peleg, the son of Eber, the son of Shelah, the son of Cainan, the son of Arphaxad, the son of Shem, the son of Noah, the son of Lamech, the son of Methuselah, the son of Enoch, the son of Jared, the son of Mahalaleel, the son of Cainan, the son of Enosh, the son of Seth, the son of Adam, the son of God.

CHAPTER 4

Jesus, full of the Holy Spirit, returned from the Jordan and was brought by the Spirit into the desert for forty days, where he was tested by the devil.[a]

During that time he ate nothing, and by the end of it he was hungry. The devil said to him, "If you are the son of God, tell this rock to become bread".

But Jesus answered him, "It is written in the Scriptures, 'Man will not live by bread alone'".

Then the devil led him up high and showed him all the kingdoms of the world in a moment of time. And the devil said to him, "I will give all this authority to you, and the glory of all these kingdoms, because it is mine to give. And I can give it to anyone I wish. If, then, you will worship me, all of it will be yours."

But Jesus replied to him, "It is written, 'You are to worship the Lord your God, and serve him alone'".

Then the devil took him to Jerusalem, stood him on the pinnacle of the temple and said to him, "If you are the son of God, throw

a The spiritual enemy of God and his people; also called 'Satan'.

yourself down from here, for it is written, 'He will command his angels concerning you, to guard you', and 'They will bear you up on their hands, in case you should strike your foot against a rock'".

Jesus answered him, "It is said, 'Do not test the Lord your God'".

And when the devil had finished every test, he left Jesus until an opportune time.

Jesus returned in the power of the Spirit to Galilee, and a report about him spread throughout the whole region. He taught in their synagogues, and everybody spoke glowingly of him.

He came to Nazareth where he had grown up, and as was his custom, he went into the synagogue on the Sabbath Day.[b] He stood up to read, and the scroll of the prophet Isaiah was handed to him. Unrolling it, he found the place where it was written, "The Spirit of the Lord is upon me, because he has anointed me to announce great news to the poor; he has sent me to proclaim release for prisoners, and sight once more for the blind, to send the oppressed away free; to proclaim the acceptable year of the Lord".

Rolling up the scroll, he gave it to the assistant and sat down. And the eyes of everyone in the synagogue were fixed on him.

He began to speak to them, "Today, this Scripture is fulfilled in your hearing".

And they were all speaking highly of him, and were amazed at the gracious words that came out of his mouth. They said, "Isn't this Joseph's son?"

And he said to them, "No doubt you will quote this proverb to me, 'Physician, heal yourself! What we have heard you did in Capernaum, do here as well in your home town.'"

But he went on, "Truly, I tell you that no prophet is acceptable in his home town. Truly, I tell you, there were many widows in Elijah's time in Israel, when the heavens were shut for three years and six months, and a great famine settled on the whole land. Elijah was sent to none of them, but only to the widow of Zarephath in Sidon. And there were many lepers in Israel in the time of Elisha the prophet, but none of them was cleansed; only Naaman the Syrian."[c]

b From sunset Friday to sunset Saturday, the day of rest set down in the Law of Moses.
c Sidon and Syria were both outside Israel.

When they heard this in the synagogue, they were all filled with rage. Rising up, they ran him out of the city, and led him to the edge of the cliff on which their city was built, in order to throw him down. But he passed straight through their midst, and went on his way.

Then he went down to Capernaum, which was a city in Galilee, and he taught them on the Sabbath Day. They were astonished at his teaching, because he spoke with authority.

Now in the synagogue there was a man with an unclean demonic spirit, and he called out in a loud voice, "Hey! What have you to do with us, Jesus of Nazareth? Have you come to destroy us? I know who you are: the holy one of God!"

Jesus rebuked him, and said, "Be silent, and come out of him". And after hurling the man down in their midst, the demon came out of him. The man was unharmed.

They were all awestruck, and said to one another, "What sort of word is this, that he commands the unclean spirits with authority and power, and they come out?"

And reports about him spread throughout the whole region.

Jesus stood up and left the synagogue, and went to Simon's house. Simon's mother-in-law was in the grip of a high fever, and they asked him to do something for her.

Jesus stood over her and rebuked the fever, and it left her. She got straight up and began to serve them.

As the sun was setting, everyone who had any who were sick with various diseases brought them to him. He laid his hands on each one of them, and healed them. And demons came out of many people, calling out, "You are the son of God!" Yet Jesus rebuked them, and would not allow them to speak, because they knew that he was the Christ.

When it was day, he went out into a place in the desert, and the crowds were looking for him. But he said to them, "It is essential that I announce the good news of the kingdom of God to the other cities as well, because that is why I was sent".

And he went on preaching in the synagogues of Galilee.

CHAPTER 5

On one occasion, he was standing by Lake Galilee and the crowd was pressing in on him to hear the message of God. He saw two boats on the edge of the lake, left there by the fishermen who were cleaning the nets. He got into one of the boats, which belonged to Simon, and asked him to put out a little way from the land. When he had sat down, he taught the crowd from the boat.

When he had finished speaking, he said to Simon, "Go out into the deeper water, and let down your nets for a catch".

Simon answered, "Master, we have been working hard all night without getting a thing. But if you say so, I will let down the nets."

Having done so, they netted a huge quantity of fish, and their nets began to tear. They waved to their partners in the other boat to come and help them, and they came and filled both boats to the point of sinking.

Seeing all this, Simon Peter[a] fell at Jesus' knees and said, "Go away from me, Lord, for I am a sinful man". For he was gripped with fearful amazement (as were all those with him) at the catch of fish they had taken. James and John, the sons of Zebedee, who were Simon's partners, felt the same. And Jesus said to Simon, "Don't be afraid. From now on, you will catch people."

After they had brought the boats to shore, they left everything, and followed him.

In one of the towns Jesus was visiting, there was a man covered with leprosy. When he saw Jesus, he fell down before him and begged him, "Lord, if you are willing, you can make me clean".

Jesus stretched out his hand and touched him, and said, "I am willing. Be clean." And immediately the leprosy left him. Jesus commanded the man not to tell anyone. "Instead, go and show yourself to the priest, and make an offering for your purification, as Moses commanded. This will be a testimony to them."

But reports about him spread all the more, and great crowds gathered to hear him and to be healed from their sicknesses.

But he used to withdraw into the desert and pray.

a   Jesus gave Simon the additional name 'Peter'.

One day, Jesus was teaching, and some Pharisees[b] and teachers of the Law[c] were sitting there. They had come from all the towns of Galilee and Judea and Jerusalem. And the power of the Lord was with him to heal.

Some men arrived carrying a paralysed man on a stretcher. They were trying to bring him in to put him before Jesus, but because of the crowd, they could find no way through. They went up onto the roof of the house, and lowered him down on his stretcher through the tiles, right into the midst in front of Jesus. When Jesus saw their faith, he said, "Man, your sins are forgiven".

The scribes and Pharisees began to think to themselves, "Who is this who speaks such blasphemies?[d] Who is able to forgive sins except God alone?"

But Jesus knew what they were thinking, and answered them, "Why do you think this way in your hearts? Which is easier: to say, 'Your sins are forgiven' or to say, 'Get up and walk'? But so that you may know that the Son of Man[e] has authority in the land to forgive sins …" He said to the paralysed man, "I say to you, get up, and pick up your stretcher and go back home".

And immediately he got up right there in front of them, picked up what he had been lying on and went back to his home, giving honour and praise to God.

Everybody was stunned, and honoured and praised God. They were quite afraid, and said, "We have seen extraordinary things today".

After this, Jesus went out and saw a tax collector named Levi sitting at the tax collecting booth. He said to him, "Follow me", and he got up, left everything, and followed him. And Levi held a great feast for Jesus at his house, with a large crowd of tax collectors; and others were there as well, reclining at the table with them.[f]

b A strict religious group among the Jews who emphasised keeping the law in every detail.

c Also described in Luke as 'scribes' and 'experts in the law'.

d That is, offensive words spoken against God, such as claiming to be equal with God.

e 'Son of Man' was a common Jewish way of referring to oneself in the third person (as 'oneself' is in English). Jesus also used this expression to refer back to an exalted figure in Old Testament prophecy, the 'Son of Man' of Daniel 7, who is given all authority by God.

f People did not sit on chairs to eat in the ancient world; they had low tables, and reclined on cushions or couches to eat.

Now the Pharisees and scribes complained to Jesus' disciples,[g] "Why do you eat and drink with tax collectors and sinners?"

And Jesus replied, "It is not the healthy who need a doctor, but the sick. I have not come to invite the righteous, but sinners to repentance."

They said to him, "John's disciples are often fasting and praying, and so are the disciples of the Pharisees. But yours eat and drink!"

Jesus replied, "Are you able to make wedding guests fast while the bridegroom is with them? But the days will come when the bridegroom is taken away from them, and then they will fast."

He also told them this parable:[h] "No-one tears a piece off a new garment and sews it onto an old one—you would not only have torn the new one, but the patch from the new would not match the old. And no-one pours young wine into old wineskins—the young wine would burst the wineskins, the wine would spill everywhere, and the wineskins would be ruined. But young wine must go into new wineskins. And no-one, having drunk old wine, wants young wine; for he says, 'The old is good.'"

CHAPTER 6

One Sabbath Day while he was walking through the grain fields, his disciples were plucking the heads of grain, rubbing them in their hands, and eating them. Some of the Pharisees said, "Why are you doing what is unlawful on the Sabbath?"

Jesus answered them by saying, "Haven't you read what David did when he and his men were hungry? He went into the house of God, took the special bread for the offering, and ate it; and he gave some to those who were with him. And this was the bread that was unlawful to eat, except for the priests alone." He said to them, "The Son of Man is Lord of the Sabbath".

On another Sabbath Day, he went into the synagogue to teach. And a man was there with a deformed right hand. The scribes and Pharisees were watching Jesus in case he healed on

g A 'disciple' is someone who follows and learns from a teacher.
h A short proverbial saying or story or riddle.

the Sabbath, so that they could accuse him.

But Jesus knew what they were thinking. He said to the man with the deformed hand, "Get up and stand here in the middle". And he rose and stood there.

Jesus said to them, "Let me ask you, on the Sabbath is it lawful to do good or to do evil? To save life or destroy?" Looking round at all of them, he said to the man, "Stretch out your hand". He did so, and his hand was restored.

This made them furious, and they began to discuss with one another what they might do to Jesus.

Around that time, he went out to the mountain to pray, and spent all night in prayer to God. When it was day, he summoned his disciples, and chose twelve of them, whom he called apostles.[a] There was Simon (also called Peter), Andrew his brother, James, John, Philip, Bartholomew, Matthew, Thomas, James (son of Alphaeus), Simon (called the Zealot), Judas (son of James) and Judas Iscariot, who became a traitor.

He went down with them to a level place, along with a great crowd of his disciples. And a huge number of people from all over Judea and Jerusalem and the coastal region of Tyre and Sidon came to hear him and to be healed of their diseases. Those who were troubled by unclean spirits were also being healed. The whole crowd was trying to touch him, because power came from him and was healing everyone.

Then he turned his attention to his disciples, and said,

"Blessed are you who are poor, because the kingdom of God belongs to you.

"Blessed are you who are hungry now, because you will be fed.

"Blessed are you who weep now, because you will laugh.

"Blessed are you when people hate you and reject you and criticise you and blacken your name on account of the Son of Man. Rejoice and leap for joy in that day, for great is your reward in heaven; for the ancestors of those who persecute you used to do the same to the prophets.

a 'Apostle' literally means 'one sent out (for a task)'. In the New Testament, it usually refers to those sent out to continue Jesus' preaching.

"But, woe to you who are rich, because you are receiving your comfort.

"Woe to you who are full now, because you will be hungry.

"Woe to you who laugh now, because you will mourn and weep.

"Woe to you when everyone speaks well of you, for their ancestors used to do the same to the false prophets.

"But to you who are listening, I say: love your enemies. Do good to those who hate you. Bless those who curse you. Pray for those who mistreat you. If someone strikes you on the cheek, offer him the other cheek as well; and if someone takes your coat, let him have your shirt as well. To everyone who asks of you, give; and if someone takes your things, don't demand them back. And in the way you want people to treat you, do the same for them.

"If you love those who love you, what credit is that to you? For even the sinners love those who love them. And if you do good to those who do good to you, what credit is that to you? Even the sinners do that. And if you lend to those you know will return the favour, what credit is that to you? Even sinners lend to sinners so that they might receive as much back.

"But love your enemies, and do good and lend without expecting anything back. Your reward will be great, and you will be sons of the Most High,[b] because he shows kindness to the ungrateful and the immoral. Be merciful, as your Father is merciful. And do not judge, or else you also will be judged. Do not condemn, or else you also will be condemned. Forgive, and you will be forgiven. Give, and it will be given to you—a good amount, pressed down, shaken and running over, will be put in your lap—for the amount you give will be the amount you get back."

He also told them a parable: "Can the blind lead the blind? Will they not both fall into a ditch? The student is not above the teacher; but everyone who has been fully trained will be like his teacher.

"Why do you notice the speck that is in your brother's eye, but do not consider the log that is in your own? How can you possibly say to your brother, 'Brother, let me take the speck out of your eye', when you haven't noticed the log in your own eye?

b To 'be sons of' was a Jewish way of saying you were like someone or something; that you bore the family likeness.

You hypocrite! First take the log out of your own eye, and then you will be able to see clearly to remove the speck from your brother's eye.

"For a good tree never produces bad fruit; nor does a bad tree produce good fruit, because each tree is known by its own fruit. Figs are not gathered from thorn bushes, nor are grapes picked from bramble bushes. A good person brings out good things from the good treasure of his heart; and an evil person brings forth evil from the evil in his heart. For his mouth speaks from the overflow of the heart.

"Why do you call me 'Lord, Lord', but do not do what I say? Everyone who comes to me and hears my message and puts it into practice—let me show you what that person is like: he is like a man who was building a house, and who dug down deep and laid the foundation on solid rock. When a flood came, the river burst upon that house, but could not shake it, because the house was well built. However, the person who hears my message but does not put it into practice is like a man who built a house on the soil, without a foundation. And when the river burst upon it, the house collapsed immediately, and its destruction was total."

CHAPTER 7

After Jesus had completed all his teachings in the hearing of the people, he entered Capernaum. Now a certain centurion[a] had a highly-valued servant, who was ill to the point of death. When the centurion heard about Jesus, he sent some Jewish elders to ask him whether he could come, so that the servant might be healed.

When they came to Jesus they strongly urged him, saying, "This man is worthy of your help, for he loves our nation and he built our synagogue".

So Jesus went with them. When he was not far from the house, the centurion sent friends to say to him, "Lord, do not trouble yourself, for I do not deserve to have you come under my roof. And neither did I count myself worthy to come to see you.

a   A Roman army officer in charge of a hundred men.

But say the word and my servant will be healed. For I too am a man under authority, and I have soldiers under me. I say to this one, 'Go' and he goes, and to another 'Come here' and he comes, and to my servant, 'Do this', and he does it."

When he heard this, Jesus was amazed at him, and turning to the crowd that was following him, said, "I tell you, not even in Israel have I found faith like this!"

And those who had been sent to Jesus returned to the house, and found the servant well again.

Not long afterwards, Jesus went to a city called Nain, and his disciples and a large crowd went with him. As he drew near the gate of the city, he saw that they were carrying out a dead person, who was the only son of his widowed mother. A crowd from the city was with the widow. When he saw her, the Lord had compassion for her, and said, "Don't cry". And he stepped forward and laid his hand on the coffin. The pall-bearers stood still, and he said, "Young man, I say to you, rise up!"

The dead man sat up and began to speak, and Jesus gave him to his mother.

Fear took hold of everyone, and they glorified God, saying, "A great prophet has arisen amongst us" and "God has visited his people". And this report about him spread through all of Judea and the surrounding region.

John's disciples told him about all these things. So John selected two of his disciples, and sent them to the Lord to ask, "Are you the Coming One, or should we wait for another?" The men came to Jesus and said, "John the Baptist sent us to you to ask, 'Are you the Coming One, or should we wait for another?'"

At that particular time, Jesus healed many people from illnesses and diseases and evil spirits, and he gave many blind people back their sight. He answered the men, "Go back and tell John what you see and hear: the blind see, the crippled walk, and the lepers are being cleansed; the deaf hear, the dead are being raised, and the poor are hearing the great news. And blessed is the one who does not stumble because of me."

When John's messengers had gone, he began to talk to the

crowd about John: "What did you go out into the desert to see? A reed being shaken by the wind? What did you go out to see? A man dressed in fine clothes? No, those who have gorgeous clothes and luxuries live in royal palaces. So what did you go out to see? A prophet? Yes, I tell you, and much more than a prophet. He is the one about whom it is written in the Scriptures, 'See, I send my messenger before you, who will prepare your way before you'. I tell you, among those born of women, none is greater than John; but the person who is least in the kingdom of God is greater than him!"

(And when all the people heard this, including the tax collectors, they considered God's actions to be just, since they had been baptised with John's baptism. However, the Pharisees and religious lawyers, who had not been baptised by him, rejected God's purpose for themselves.)

"To what, then, shall I compare the people of this generation? What are they like? They are like children sitting in the marketplace, calling out to one another, 'We played the flute for you and you didn't dance; we wailed and you didn't weep'. For John the Baptist came neither eating bread nor drinking wine, and you say, 'He has a demon!' The Son of Man came eating and drinking, and you say, 'Look, he's a glutton and a drunkard, a friend of tax collectors and sinners'. Yet wisdom is considered just by all her children."

One of the Pharisees invited Jesus to dine with him, and Jesus went to the Pharisee's house, and reclined at the table. Now there was a woman in the city who was a sinner, and when she found out that Jesus was having dinner at the Pharisee's house, she brought an alabaster jar of perfumed lotion. She stood behind Jesus, near his feet, crying; and her tears began to wet his feet, and she started to wipe his feet with her hair and to kiss them, and to anoint them with the lotion.

When the Pharisee who invited Jesus saw this, he said to himself, "If this man was really a prophet, he would realise who she was and what kind of woman was touching him—that she is a sinner".

And Jesus answered him, "Simon, I have something to say to you".

"Teacher," he said, "go ahead and speak".

"There were two people in debt to a certain money-lender. One owed him the equivalent of five hundred days' wages; the other fifty. Neither of them was able to pay, and so the money-lender forgave both debts. Which of them, then, will love him more?"

Simon answered, "I suppose the one who was forgiven more".

He said to him, "You have judged rightly".

And turning to the woman, he said to Simon, "Do you see this woman? I came into your house—you did not provide water for my feet; but she has been wetting my feet with her tears and wiping them with her hair. You gave me no kiss; but from the time I arrived she has not stopped kissing my feet. You did not anoint my head with oil; but she has anointed my feet with lotion. And so I say to you, she has had many sins forgiven; that is why she loves much. But he who is forgiven little, loves little."

He said to her, "Your sins are forgiven".

And those who were reclining at the table with him began to say to themselves, "Who is this, who even forgives sins?"

He said to the woman, "Your faith has rescued you; go in peace".

CHAPTER 8

Soon after this, Jesus travelled through the towns and villages, preaching and announcing the great news of the kingdom of God, and the twelve apostles were with him. Certain women who had been healed of evil spirits and illnesses were also with him—Mary who was called Magdalene (from whom seven demons had been cast out), Joanna (the wife of Herod's steward Chuza), Susanna, and many others. These women supported them financially.

A great crowd gathered, coming to him from every town. So he told a parable:

"A sower went out to sow his seed. And while he was sowing, some of the seed fell along the path and was trampled on, and the birds ate it. Other seed fell on rocky ground, and as soon as it grew it withered, because it had no moisture. Still other seed fell in the midst of thorns, and the thorns grew up alongside, and choked it. But other seed fell in good soil, and having grown, it produced a massive crop." After saying this, he called out, "Let anyone with ears to hear, listen!"

His disciples asked him what this parable meant. He said to them, "You have been granted to know the secrets of the kingdom of God, but for the rest it is all in parables, so that even though they are 'seeing' they may not see, and even though they are 'hearing' they may not understand. This is what the parable means: The seed is the message of God. The seed that fell along the path represents those who hear, but then the devil comes and takes the message from their heart, so that they may not believe and be rescued. The seed that fell on the rocky ground stands for those who, when they hear, receive the message with joy. But they do not have any root. They believe for a while, but when the time of testing comes, they leave.

"Now the seed that fell into the thorns represents those who hear, but as they go along, they are choked by the worries and riches and pleasures of life; and they never mature to produce fruit. And the seed that fell in good soil—these are the people who hear the message, and hold onto it in their good and noble hearts, and, in persevering, produce fruit.

"No-one after lighting a lamp covers it with a bowl or puts it under the bed, but places it on a lampstand, so that those who come in might see the light. For there is nothing hidden that will not become plain, and nothing concealed that will not become known and come to light. Be careful, then, how you listen. For whoever has, more will be given to him; but whoever does not have, even what he seems to have will be taken away from him."

Jesus' mother and brothers arrived to see him, but they were not able to reach him because of the crowd. And someone told him, "Your mother and brothers are standing outside, wanting to see you". Jesus replied, "These are my mother and brothers—those who hear the message of God and put it into practice".

One day, he got into a boat with his disciples and said to them, "Let us go across to the other side of the lake". They set out, and while they were sailing, he fell asleep. Then a windstorm came down the lake. The boat was filling with water and they were in real danger.

They went and woke Jesus and said, "Master, Master, we are dying!" But he got up and rebuked the wind and the raging water, and they stopped, and it became calm.

He said to the disciples, "Where is your faith?" They were afraid and astonished, and said to one another, "Who then is this, that he commands even the winds and the water, and they obey him?"

They sailed on to the country of the Gerasenes, which is on the shore opposite Galilee. When he got out of the boat, he was met by a certain man from the city, who had demons. For a long time he had not worn clothes, and instead of living in a house, he lived among the tombs.

When he saw Jesus, he cried out and fell down before him, and said in a loud voice, "What have I got to do with you, Jesus, son of the Most High God? I beg you, do not torture me." For Jesus had commanded the unclean spirit to come out of the man. Many times it had seized him, and he used to be bound with chains and shackles, and kept under guard. But he would break the bonds, and be driven by the demon into the desert.

Jesus asked him, "What is your name?" And he replied, "Legion", because many demons had gone into him. And they pleaded with him not to order them to depart into the abyss.[a]

Now there was a good-sized herd of pigs grazing on the hillside. The demons begged him to permit them to enter the pigs, and he allowed them to do so. The demons left the man and went into the pigs, and the herd rushed over the cliff into the lake and was drowned.

When those who were looking after the pigs saw this, they fled, and reported it to those in the city and in the country, who then came out to see what had happened. They came to Jesus and found the man from whom the demons had been driven out sitting at Jesus' feet, clothed and in his right mind. And they were afraid. Those who had seen it all explained how the demon-

a The deep underworld home of demons.

possessed man had been healed.[b]

Then all those from the region of the Gerasenes asked him to go away from them, for they were gripped with great fear. And getting back into the boat, he returned across the lake.

The man from whom the demons had come out begged to go with him, but Jesus sent him away, saying, "Go back to your home, and tell what God has done for you". And he went through the whole city, declaring what Jesus had done for him.

When Jesus returned, a crowd was there to welcome him, for they had all been waiting for him. A man named Jairus, who was a ruler of the synagogue, came straight up to Jesus and fell at his feet, and begged him to come to his house. The reason was that his only daughter, who was about twelve years old, was dying.

While Jesus was on his way, the crowds almost crushed him. Among them was a woman who had suffered from a flow of blood for twelve years, and no-one had been able to cure her, though she had spent all her resources on doctors. Coming up behind Jesus, she touched the fringe of his clothes, and immediately the flow of blood ceased.

Jesus said, "Who touched me?" They all denied it, and Peter said, "Master, the crowds are pressing in and crushing you".

But Jesus said, "Someone touched me, for I know that power has gone out from me".

When the woman saw that she could not stay hidden, she came trembling and fell down before him. And she declared before everyone why she had touched him, and how she had been instantly healed.

He said to her, "Daughter, your faith has healed[b] you. Go in peace."

While he was still speaking, someone came from the synagogue ruler's house and said to Jairus, "Your daughter is dead. Do not trouble the teacher any longer."

Jesus heard this, and said to him, "Don't be afraid; only have faith and she will be healed".[b]

When he came to the house, he let no-one go in with him

b Or 'saved', or 'rescued'.

except Peter, James and John, and the girl's father and mother. Everyone was weeping and mourning for her, but he said, "Do not weep. For she is not dead, only sleeping." And they laughed at him, because they knew she had died.

Jesus grasped her hand, and called out, "Child, rise up!"

Her spirit returned and she sat up immediately; and he ordered that she be given something to eat.

Her parents were astounded, and he commanded them not to say what had happened.

CHAPTER 9

He called together the twelve, and gave them power and authority over all the demons, and to heal sicknesses. And he sent them out to proclaim the kingdom of God and to heal the sick. He said to them, "Take nothing for the journey—no staff, no bag, no bread, no money, not even a spare shirt. And whatever house you enter, stay there until you leave. Wherever they do not welcome you, shake the dust off your feet as you leave that city, as a testimony against them."

They set out, and went through the towns announcing the great news, and healing everywhere.

Now Herod the tetrarch heard about all these happenings. He was perplexed, because it was being said by some that John the Baptist had been raised from the dead, and by others that Elijah had appeared; and others were saying that an ancient prophet had risen up.

Herod said, "John I beheaded; but who is this man I am hearing these things about?" And he tried to see him.

When the apostles returned, they reported to Jesus what they had done. And taking them with him, he withdrew privately to a town called Bethsaida.

But the crowds found out, and followed him. He welcomed them, and spoke to them about the kingdom of God, and cured those who were in need of healing. The day was drawing to a close, and the twelve came and said to him, "Send the crowd away, so that they can go into the surrounding towns and fields to lodge, and to find food—because we are in a desert".

But Jesus said to them, "Give them something to eat yourselves".

They said, "We don't have more than five loaves of bread and two fish; unless perhaps we should go and buy provisions for all these people!" (for there were about five thousand men).

He said to his disciples, "Sit them down in groups of fifty". And they did so, and the crowd all sat down.

Taking the five loaves and two fish, Jesus looked up to heaven, blessed them, broke them, and kept giving them to the disciples to set before the crowd. And they ate and were all satisfied. The leftovers were gathered up, and there were twelve baskets of broken pieces.

Once, while he was praying alone, with his disciples close by, he asked them a question: "Who do the crowds say that I am?"

And they answered, "John the Baptist; others say Elijah, and others that an ancient prophet has risen up".

He said to them, "And you, who do you say I am?"

Peter answered, "The Christ of God".

And he sternly commanded them not to say this to anyone, saying, "The Son of Man must suffer many things, and be rejected by the elders and chief priests and scribes, and be killed, and on the third day be raised up".

He said to them all, "If anyone wants to come after me, let him deny himself and pick up his cross[a] each day, and follow me. For whoever wants to save his life will lose it; but whoever loses his life for my sake—he will save it. For what profit does a person get if he gains the whole world, but loses or forfeits his very self? For whoever is ashamed of me and my words, the Son of Man will be ashamed of him when he comes in his glory and in the glory of the Father and the holy angels. I tell you the truth, there are some standing here who will not taste death until they see the kingdom of God."

a The cross was a brutal Roman method of execution, in which prisoners were tied or nailed to an upright wooden cross and left to die (eventually from not being able to lift themselves up to breathe). Prisoners usually had to carry their crosses to the place of execution.

About eight days after he had said these things, Jesus took Peter, John and James up to the mountain to pray. As he was praying, the appearance of his face changed, and his clothing became white like lightning. Suddenly two men were there speaking with him—Moses and Elijah. They appeared in brilliant glory, and spoke about his departure, which he was about to complete in Jerusalem.

Now Peter and those with him were drowsy with sleep, but they woke up and saw his glory, and the two men who were standing with him. And when they were starting to separate from Jesus to leave, Peter said to him, "Master, it is good that we are here. Let us make three tents—one for you, and one for Moses, and one for Elijah". (He didn't know what he was saying.)

While Peter was still saying this, a cloud came and surrounded them. They were afraid as they entered the cloud, and a voice came from out of the cloud and said, "This is my Chosen One, my Son; listen to him".

And when the voice had spoken, Jesus was found alone. They kept quiet and told no-one at that time about anything they had seen.

The next day, after they had come down from the mountain, a great crowd was there to meet him. A man from the crowd cried out, "Teacher, I beg you to look at my son, because he is my only child. A spirit keeps on seizing him; it suddenly calls out and throws him into convulsions, with foaming at the mouth. It is destroying him, and hardly ever leaves him. I pleaded with your disciples to cast it out, but they were not able to."

Jesus answered, "O faithless and perverse generation, how long do I have to be with you and put up with you? Bring your son here."

While the boy was still coming forward, the demon attacked him and threw him into convulsions. But Jesus rebuked the unclean spirit and healed the boy, and returned him to his father.

They were all amazed at the majesty of God. But while they were marvelling at all the things he was doing, he said to his disciples, "Let these words sink in: the Son of Man is about to be betrayed into the hands of men". They didn't understand how this could be; indeed, it was hidden from them so that they didn't grasp it. And they were afraid to ask him what he meant.

Now a discussion arose among them as to which of them was the greatest. Knowing what they were thinking, Jesus took a child and stood him by his side. He said to the disciples, "Whoever welcomes this child in my name, welcomes me; and whoever welcomes me, welcomes the One who sent me. For he who is least among you all is the greatest."

John replied, "Master, we saw someone casting out demons in your name, and we stopped him, because he was not following with us".

But Jesus said to him, "Don't stop him. For whoever is not against you is for you."

When the time was drawing near for him to be taken up, he set himself to go to Jerusalem. He sent messengers to go before him, and they went into a Samaritan[b] town to prepare for his arrival. The Samaritans, however, would not welcome him, because he had set himself to go to Jerusalem.

When the disciples James and John saw this, they said, "Lord, do you want us to call fire down from heaven and destroy them?" But Jesus turned and rebuked them; and they went into another village.

As they went on their way, someone said to him, "I will follow you wherever you go".

But Jesus said to him, "Foxes have holes, and birds have nests, but the Son of Man has nowhere to lay his head".

Jesus said to someone else, "Follow me". But he replied, "Lord, first allow me to go and bury my father".

Jesus said to him, "Let the dead take care of the dead; but as for you, go and proclaim the kingdom of God".

Someone else also said to him, "I will follow you, Lord, but first allow me to say goodbye to my family".

Jesus replied, "No-one who puts his hand to the plough and looks back is fit for the kingdom of God".

b Samaria lay on the way south to Judea and Jerusalem from Galilee. The Samaritans had a hostile relationship with the Jews.

CHAPTER 10

After this, the Lord appointed seventy others, and sent them on before him in pairs into all the cities and towns where he was about to go. He said to them, "The harvest is large, but the workers are few; therefore, beg the Lord of the harvest to send out workers into his harvest. Go on your way. But watch out—I send you like lambs into the midst of wolves. Do not take a wallet with you, nor a bag, nor sandals; and do not greet anyone on the road. And when you enter a house, first say, 'Peace be on this house'; and if a son of peace is already there, your peace will rest on him; but if not, your word will return to you unused. Remain in his house, eating and drinking what they provide, for the worker deserves his wage. Do not go about from house to house.

"When you go into a city and they welcome you, eat what they set before you. Heal the sick there and tell them, 'The kingdom of God is near—almost upon you'. But if you enter a city and they do not welcome you, go out into its streets and say, 'We even wipe off the dust that clings to our feet from your city! But know this: the kingdom of God is near.' I say to you that it will be more tolerable for Sodom[a] on the day of judgement than for that city.

"Woe to you, Chorazin; woe to you, Bethsaida![b] For if the powerful deeds that have happened in you had taken place in Tyre and Sidon[c] long ago, they would have repented in sackcloth and ashes. But it will be more tolerable for Tyre and Sidon in the judgement than for you. And you, Capernaum, will you be lifted up to the heavens? No, you will go down to hell.

"The one who listens to you, listens to me; and the one who rejects you, rejects me. But the one who rejects me, rejects the One who sent me."

The seventy returned joyfully, saying, "Lord, even the demons submitted to us in your name!"

---

a An Old Testament city of great wickedness that was destroyed by God.
b Chorazin and Bethsaida were towns not far from Capernaum in Galilee. Capernaum was the 'home base' for much of Jesus' ministry.
c Non-Israelite cities on the eastern coast of the Mediterranean, also notorious for their evil behaviour.

And he said to them, "I was watching Satan fall, like lightning from the sky. See, I have given you authority to trample over snakes and scorpions and every power of the enemy, and absolutely nothing will harm you. But rejoice not so much that the spirits submit to you, but that your names have been written in heaven."

At that very time, he rejoiced in the Holy Spirit and said, "I thank you, Father, Lord of heaven and earth, because you have hidden these things from the wise and intelligent, and have revealed them to children. Yes, Father, because this was how it pleased you to do it. All things have been handed over to me by my Father, and no-one knows who the Son is, except the Father; or who the Father is except the Son, and all those to whom the Son decides to reveal him."

And turning to his disciples, he said to them privately, "Blessed are the eyes that see what you see. For I tell you that many prophets and kings wanted to see what you see, but never did; and to hear what you hear, but never did."

Just then, a certain expert in the Jewish law stood up, wanting to test Jesus. "Teacher," he said, "what must I do so that I will inherit eternal life?"

And he said to him, "What is written in the Law? How do you read it?"

The lawyer replied, "Love the Lord your God with all your heart and with all your soul and with all your strength and with all your mind; and love your neighbour as yourself".

Jesus said to him, "You have answered correctly. Do this, and you will live."

But the lawyer wanted to justify himself; so he said to Jesus, "And who is my neighbour?"

In reply, Jesus said, "A certain man was going from Jerusalem to Jericho, when he was ambushed by robbers. They stripped him and beat him and left him half-dead.

"Now by chance, a certain priest was going down that road, but when he saw the man he passed by on the other side.

Likewise, a Levite[d] also came to the place, but seeing the man, he passed by on the other side. Then a certain Samaritan who was travelling came to the place, and when he saw the man, he was moved with compassion. He went over to him and dressed his wounds, pouring oil and wine on them. Then the Samaritan lifted the wounded man onto his own animal, took him to an inn, and took care of him.

"The next day, he took out two days' wages and gave them to the inn-keeper, and said, 'Take care of him. And whatever more you might spend, I will pay you when I return.'

"Now which of these three, do you think, proved to be a neighbour to the man who was ambushed by robbers?"

The lawyer said, "The one who showed him mercy".

Jesus said to him, "You go and do the same".

As they were travelling, he came into a certain town. A woman named Martha welcomed him into her home, and she had a sister called Mary. Now Mary was sitting at the Lord's feet to listen to what he was saying, but Martha was worried about the many things she had to do to serve her guest. She came up and said, "Lord, don't you care that my sister is leaving me to serve on my own? Tell her to come and help me."

But the Lord answered her, "Martha, Martha, you are anxious and bothered about many things, but there is only one thing that is necessary. For Mary chose the better thing, and it will not be taken away from her."

CHAPTER 11

On one occasion, while Jesus was in a certain place and had just finished praying, one of his disciples said to him, "Lord, teach us to pray, as John taught his disciples".

He said to them, "When you pray, say:

'Father,
may your name be made holy,
may your kingdom come,

d An assistant priest in the temple.

give us each day our daily bread,
and forgive us our sins, for we ourselves forgive everyone who is indebted to us;
and do not bring us into the time of testing.'"

And he said to them, "Imagine one of you has a friend, and you go to him at midnight and say, 'Friend, lend me three loaves of bread, because my friend has arrived after a journey, and I have nothing to put before him'. And the one inside says, 'Stop disturbing me. The door is already locked, and my children are with me in bed. I can't get up and give you anything.'

"I tell you, even though he will not get up and give you bread because he is your friend, yet because of your bold persistence, he will get up and give you as much as you need.

"And so I tell you, ask and it will be given to you; seek and you will find; knock and it will be opened to you. For everyone who asks receives, and he who seeks finds, and to him who knocks, the door will be opened. If your son asks for a fish, which of you fathers will give him a snake instead? Or if he asks for an egg, will give him a scorpion? If you, then, who are evil, know how to give good gifts to your children, how much more will the Father give from heaven the Holy Spirit to those who ask him?"

Now he was driving out a demon that was mute. And as the demon came out, the man who had been mute spoke, and the crowds were astonished. But some of them said, "It is by Beelzebul, the prince of demons, that he drives out the demons". Others, wanting to test him, kept asking him to perform a sign from heaven.

But Jesus knew their thoughts, and said to them, "Every kingdom that is divided against itself comes to ruin; and every house that is against itself falls. If Satan also is divided against himself, how will his kingdom stand? For you say, 'By Beelzebul he drives out the demons', but if I drive out the demons by Beelzebul, by whom do your sons drive them out? On account of this, they will be your judges.

"However, if it is by the finger of God that I drive out the demons, then surely the kingdom of God now confronts you. When a strong, fully-armed man guards his own house, his possessions are secure. But when a stronger man comes along and defeats him, he takes from him all the armour in which he trusted, and divides up the spoils.

"He who is not with me is against me, and he who does not gather with me, scatters. Whenever an unclean spirit comes out of a person, it passes through dry places seeking rest, and does not find any. Then it says, 'I will return to the house I came out of'. And coming back, it finds it all swept clean and in order. Then it goes and gets seven other spirits more evil than itself, and goes in to live there. And that person ends up worse off than he was at the beginning."

Now while he was saying these things, a woman from the crowd shouted out, "Blessed is the womb that bore you, and the breasts that nursed you".

But Jesus said, "Blessed rather are those who hear the message of God, and keep it".

With the crowds increasing around him, he began to speak: "This generation is an evil generation. It seeks a sign; but no sign will be given to it except the sign of Jonah. For just as Jonah[a] was a sign to the Ninevites, so also the Son of Man will be to this generation. The Queen of Sheba will rise up at the judgement with the men of this generation and condemn them, because she came from the ends of the earth to hear the wisdom of Solomon.[b] Yet something greater than Solomon is here. The men of Nineveh will rise in the judgement with this generation, and condemn it, because they repented at the preaching of Jonah. Yet something greater than Jonah is here.

"No-one lights a lamp only to put it in a cellar; instead, it is put on the lampstand, so that those who enter may see its light. Your eye is the lamp of the body. When your eye is clear towards others, your whole body is full of light; but when your eye is evil,[c] then your body is dark. See to it, then, that the light within you is not darkness. If, therefore, your whole body is full of light,

---

a Jonah was an Old Testament prophet who took God's word to the people of Nineveh.

b Solomon, son of King David, was the wisest and most successful king of Israel.

c To have an 'evil eye' was a Jewish way of saying 'miserly' or 'stingy'.

with no part dark, it will be as full of light as when the lamp shines out brilliantly upon you."

While he was speaking, a Pharisee invited Jesus to have dinner with him; and Jesus went into the Pharisee's house and reclined at the table. When the Pharisee saw this, he was astonished, because Jesus did not first ritually wash himself before dinner. The Lord said to him, "Now you Pharisees cleanse the outside of the cup and the plate, but on the inside you are full of greed and wickedness. O you fools—did not he who made the outside make the inside as well? So give attention to the inside, and you will find that all things are clean for you.

"But woe to you Pharisees, because you give a tenth of your mint and rue and all your herbs, but you overlook justice and the love of God. You should have done these things, without neglecting the others.

"Woe to you Pharisees, because you love the best seat in the synagogues, and the way people greet you in the market place. Woe to you, because you are like an unmarked grave that those walking over it do not realise is there."

One of the religious lawyers answered him, "Teacher, you insult us as well by saying these things".

But Jesus said, "Woe to you religious lawyers as well! For you load people up with burdens that are hard to carry, but you yourselves will not lift one finger to bear the load. Woe to you, because you build the tombs of the prophets, but your ancestors were the ones who killed them! Therefore, you are witnesses and accomplices to the deeds of your ancestors, because they killed the prophets and you yourselves build their tombs. It is for this reason that the Wisdom of God said, 'I will send them prophets and apostles; and they will kill and persecute some of them', so that this generation might be blamed for the blood of all the prophets that has been shed since the foundation of the world— from the blood of Abel through to the blood of Zechariah,[d] who

d Abel, the son of Adam, was murdered by his brother Cain in the opening pages of the Old Testament; Zechariah, a courageous priest and prophet, was murdered near the end of the Old Testament period.

died between the altar and the sanctuary. Yes, I tell you it will be blamed on this generation!

"Woe to you experts in the Jewish law, because you hold the key to knowledge; you yourselves will not go inside, and you get in the way of those who do want to enter."

And as he left there, the scribes and Pharisees began to be very resentful, and to attack him with all kinds of questions, hoping all the time to hunt him down through something he might say.

CHAPTER 12

Meanwhile, a crowd of many thousands had gathered so that the people were actually trampling on one another.

Jesus began to speak first to his disciples: "Beware of the 'yeast' of the Pharisees, which spells hypocrisy. There is nothing that has been concealed that will not in the future be revealed, and nothing secret that will not be made known. So, whatever you have said in the dark will be heard in the light, and what you have whispered in the privacy of your home will be proclaimed from the housetops.

"To you my friends I say, do not fear those who kill the body and afterwards can do nothing more. Let me warn you about whom you should fear: fear him who, after he has killed, has authority to cast into hell. Yes, I tell you, fear him!

"Are not five sparrows sold for just a small amount? Yet not one of them is forgotten in God's sight. But even the hairs on your head have all been counted. Do not fear; you are worth more than many sparrows.

"And I tell you, everyone who acknowledges me before other people, the Son of Man will acknowledge before the angels of God. But the person who disowns me before other people will be disowned before the angels of God. And everyone who speaks a word against the Son of Man will be forgiven for it; but the one who slanders the Holy Spirit will not be forgiven.

"Now, when they bring you before the synagogues, the

leaders and the authorities, do not be anxious about how or by what you will defend yourselves, or what you will say. For the Holy Spirit will instruct you in that moment about the things you should say."

Then someone out of the crowd said to him, "Teacher, tell my brother to divide the family inheritance with me".

But Jesus said to him, "Sir, who appointed me as judge or referee for both of you?" And he said to the crowd, "Watch out and be on your guard against every type of greed, because your life isn't made up of how many things you own".

And then he told them a parable: "The land of a certain wealthy man produced a good harvest, and he thought to himself, 'What will I do, since I have nowhere to store my crops?' Then he said, 'This is what I will do. I will knock down my existing barns and build bigger ones, and there I will store all my grain and goods. And I will say to my soul, "Soul, you have many good things laid up for many years to come. Relax; eat, drink and celebrate."'

"But God said to him, 'You fool! This very night your soul is demanded back from you. And the things you have prepared—whose will they be then?'

"This is how it will be with those who store up things for themselves, but are not rich towards God."

Then he said to the disciples, "Therefore I tell you, do not be anxious about your life—what you will eat; nor about your body—what you will wear. For your life is more than food, and your body is more than clothing. Think of the crows and how they do not sow or harvest; nor do they have a storehouse or a barn, and yet God provides for them. How much more valuable you are than the birds! And which of you, by your anxiety, can add a single moment to your life span? So if you cannot achieve such a small thing, why are you anxious about the rest? Think about how the lilies grow. They do not work or make clothes. But I tell you, not even King Solomon in all his glory was dressed like one of these. Now if this is the way God clothes the grass in the field, which grows today and is thrown into the incinerator tomorrow, how much more will he clothe you—people of little faith!

"And do not strive after what you will eat and drink, or be worried. For these are the things all the nations of the world strive after, and your Father knows that you need them. Instead, strive for his kingdom, and these other things will be given to you as well. Do not fear, little flock, for it is your Father's good pleasure to give you the kingdom.

"Sell your possessions and give to the poor. Make for yourselves money bags that will not wear out; a never-ending treasure in heaven, where no thief comes close, and no moth destroys. For where your 'treasure' is, that's where your heart will be also.

"Be dressed ready for action and have your lamps lit; be like people who are expecting their master to return from a wedding banquet, so that when he comes and knocks on the door they open it immediately.

"Blessed are those servants whom the master finds alert when he returns. Truly I tell you, he will dress himself ready to work, have them recline at the table and wait on them! Blessed are those servants, if he comes at midnight or four in the morning and finds them alert.

"Now understand this: if the householder had known what time the thief would come, he would not have let him break into the house. You also be ready, because at a time you would not imagine, the Son of Man will come."

Peter said, "Lord, are you telling this parable for us or for everyone?"

The Lord replied, "Who, then, is the faithful and prudent manager whom the master will appoint over his staff to give them a food allowance at the proper time? Blessed is that servant whom the master finds doing this task when he comes. Truly I say to you, he will appoint that one over all his possessions. But if that servant says in his heart, 'My master is delayed in coming', and so begins to beat the other servants and maids, and to eat and drink and get drunk, then that servant's master will arrive on a day he does not expect, and at an hour he does not know. The master will cut him in pieces and allocate him a place with the unfaithful.

"That servant who knows his master's wishes and does not prepare for or perform his wishes will receive a great beating. But the one who does not know his wishes and yet does what is worthy of punishment will receive a light beating. From everyone who has been given much, much will be expected. And from the one who has been entrusted with much, even more will be asked.

"I have come to cast fire upon the earth, and how I wish it were burning already. I have a 'baptism' to experience and how distressed I am until it is achieved. Do you suppose that I have come to establish peace in the world? No, I tell you, but rather division! From now on, five people in one home will be divided: three against two, and two against three; they will be divided, father against son, and son against father, mother against daughter, and daughter against mother, mother-in-law against her daughter-in-law, and daughter-in-law against mother-in-law."

He also said to the crowds, "When you see a cloud rising in the west, immediately you say, 'A rainstorm is coming', and so it does. And when a south wind blows you say, 'A heat-wave will come', and so it does. You hypocrites! You know how to interpret the appearance of the earth and sky, but why don't you know how to interpret the current time? Why also do you not judge for yourselves what is right? So as you are going with your opponent to the ruler, make an effort to settle things with him, so that he will not drag you off to the judge, and the judge hand you over to the guard, and the guard throw you into prison. I say to you, you will certainly not get out from there until you have repaid the very last coin!"

CHAPTER 13

Some of those present at that time told Jesus about the people from Galilee whose blood Pilate[a] had mixed with their sacrifices. Jesus responded, "Do you think that these Galileans were worse sinners than all the other Galileans because they suffered these

a That is, Pontius Pilate, the Roman Governor of Judea.

things? No, I tell you, but if you do not repent, you will all perish as they did. Or those eighteen people upon whom the tower in Siloam fell and killed them—do you think that they were more guilty than all the other people living in Jerusalem? No, I tell you, but if you do not repent, you will all perish just as they did."

Then he told this parable: "A man had a fig tree planted in his vineyard; and he came looking for fruit on it but found none. Then he said to the gardener, 'Look, I have come looking for fruit on this fig tree for three years, yet I still find none. Cut it down. Why should it even waste the soil?' But the gardener answered, 'Lord, please leave it for one more year, until I can dig around it and fertilise it. It may yet produce fruit; but if it does not, by all means, cut it down.'"

Now Jesus was teaching in one of the synagogues on the Sabbath Day. There was a woman there who had suffered from a spirit of weakness for eighteen years; she was doubled over and unable to stand up straight. When Jesus saw her, he called her over and said, "Dear woman, be released from your weakness". He laid his hands on her and immediately she straightened up and began honouring and praising God.

But the synagogue-leader was very annoyed that Jesus had healed on the Sabbath Day, and responded by saying to the crowd, "There are six days on which work should be done, so come and be healed on one of those days, not on the Sabbath Day!"

But the Lord replied, "You hypocrites! Doesn't each of you release your ox or donkey from the feeding trough on the Sabbath, and lead it away for a drink? This woman is a daughter of Abraham. She has been imprisoned by Satan for eighteen years. Should she not be released from this prison on the Sabbath Day?"

As he said these things, those who opposed him were humiliated, yet the entire crowd was overjoyed because of the wonderful things he was doing.

So he said, "What is the kingdom of God like and to what shall I compare it? It is like a mustard seed that someone took and threw into his garden. It grew and became a tree, and the birds of the air nested in its branches." Again he said, "To what shall I compare the kingdom of God? It is like yeast that a woman took and mixed into a large amount of flour until the whole batch of dough was leavened."

Jesus was travelling through various cities and towns, teaching in them, as he continued his journey toward Jerusalem. And someone asked him, "Lord, will only a small number of people be rescued?"

He replied to them, "Strive to enter through the narrow door. For, I tell you, once the owner of the house gets up and locks the door, many will try to enter but not be able to. You will stand outside and begin to knock on the door, saying, 'Lord, open up for us!' But he will say in reply, 'I do not know where you come from'. Then you will begin to say, 'We ate and drank with you and you taught in our streets'. But he will say to you, 'I do not know where you come from. Get away from me, all of you doers of injustice!' In that place there will be weeping and grinding of teeth, when you see Abraham and Isaac and Jacob and all the prophets inside the kingdom of God, but you yourselves thrown out of it. Yet people from east and west, from north and south, will come and recline at the dining table in the kingdom of God. Indeed, some who are now last will be first, and some who are now first will be last."

At that very time, some Pharisees came to Jesus saying, "Depart from here and move on, because King Herod is looking to kill you".

He replied, "Go tell that fox, 'Listen, I will continue to cast out demons and perform healings today and tomorrow, and on the third day I will complete my goal. But I must keep moving on today and tomorrow and the next day, because it is unthinkable that a prophet would be killed outside of Jerusalem.'

"Jerusalem, Jerusalem, the city that kills the prophets and stones those sent to her! How often I have wanted to gather your children together as a hen gathers her own chicks under her wing, yet you were not willing. Look, your house is left abandoned. I tell you, you will not see me until the time comes when you declare, 'Blessed is the one who comes in the name of the Lord'."

CHAPTER 14

One Sabbath Day, Jesus was going to the home of a leading Pharisee to eat a meal, and they were watching him closely. Just then, a man came to him who was suffering from oedema.[a] Jesus asked the experts in the Jewish law and the Pharisees, "Is it lawful to heal on the Sabbath or not?" But they kept silent. So Jesus took hold of the man, healed him, and helped him on his way.

Then he said to them, "If your son or your ox fell into a pit on the Sabbath, who among you would not pull him out straight away?" And they were not able to give a reply to this.

At the meal, he noticed how the guests all chose to sit at the places of honour. So he told them a parable: "When you are invited by someone to a wedding reception, do not recline at the places of honour in case someone more honoured than you has been invited by the host. The one who invited you both may come and say to you, 'Give this person your place'. And then in disgrace you will move to the lowest place. But when you are invited, make your way to the lowest place, so that when your host comes he may say to you, 'Friend, move up to a more honourable place'. Then you will be honoured before everyone sitting at the table with you. For everyone who lifts himself up will be humbled, and the one who humbles himself will be lifted up."

Then Jesus said to his host, "When you put on a dinner or a banquet, do not call your friends or your colleagues or your family members or wealthy neighbours, in case they return the invitation and you would be repaid. Instead, when you put on a banquet, invite the poor, the disabled, the crippled and the blind. Then you will be blessed because they do not have the means to repay you. Indeed, you will be repaid at the resurrection of the righteous."[b]

On hearing this, one of those at the table said to Jesus, "Blessed is the person who will share a meal in the kingdom of God".

So Jesus said to him, "A certain man organised a feast and invited many guests. When it was time for the feast, he sent his servant to say to the guests, 'Come along, for the meal is now ready'. One after

a A medical condition characterised by an excess of watery fluid causing swelling.
b Another way of describing the day of judgement, when everyone will rise from the dead and stand before God.

another, they all began to make excuses. The first one said to him, 'I have just bought a field and I must go out to see it. Please have me excused.' Another said, 'I have just bought five pairs of oxen and I am going to inspect them. Please have me excused.' Another said, 'I have just married a wife and so am not able to attend'. The servant went back and reported these things to his master.

"The master of the home was furious and said to his servant, 'Go out quickly into the streets and lanes of the city and bring in the poor, the disabled, the blind and lame'.

"Then the servant said, 'Master, what you ordered has been done, yet there is still some room'.

"The master said to the servant, 'Go out into the highways and country lanes and convince them to come in, so that my house may be filled. For I tell you, not one of those people I previously invited will taste my feast'."

Now, great crowds of people were travelling along with Jesus. He turned around and said to them, "If anyone comes to me and does not hate his own father, mother, wife, children, brothers and sisters, and even his own life, he is not able to be my disciple. Whoever does not carry his own cross and come after me is not able to be my disciple. For who among you would plan to build a tower and not first sit down and calculate the cost; whether you have enough to complete it? Otherwise, you may lay the foundation and not be able to finish it. And everyone who sees it would begin to mock you: 'This person began to build yet is unable to finish it'. Or what king would go out to meet another king in battle, and not first sit down to consider whether he is able with ten thousand soldiers to confront the one who brings twenty thousand against him? If he is not able, then while the other is still far away he would send out representatives to ask for terms of peace. Therefore, in the same way, every one of you who does not give up all that you have is not able to be my disciple.

"So then, salt is good; but if it becomes tasteless, how can it possibly be made salty again? It is not suitable for the soil or the compost heap; people simply throw it away. Let anyone with ears to hear, listen!"

CHAPTER 15

Now all the tax collectors and sinners were gathering near to listen to Jesus. But the Pharisees and the scribes were grumbling and saying, "This man welcomes sinners and eats meals with them". So he told them this parable:

"What man among you, if he owned a hundred sheep and lost one of them, would not leave the ninety-nine in the desert and go after the lost one until he found it? And when he had found it, he would carry it upon his shoulders and be overjoyed. Returning home, he would call together his friends and neighbours and say to them, 'Rejoice with me because I have found my lost sheep!' I tell you, in the same way there will be more joy in heaven over one sinner who repents than over ninety-nine righteous people who do not need repentance.

"Or again, what woman, if she owned ten silver coins and lost one of them, would not light a lamp, sweep her home, and search thoroughly until she found it? And when she found it, she would call together her friends and neighbours and say, 'Rejoice with me because I have found the lost silver coin!' In the same way, I tell you, there is joy in the presence of God's angels over one sinner who repents."

Jesus continued: "There was a man who had two sons. The younger one said to his father, 'Father, give me my share of the inheritance'. The father then divided the property between the two sons. Soon afterwards, the younger son collected everything together and travelled to a distant land, where he squandered his inheritance on reckless living. After he had spent everything, there was a great famine in that land, and he began to be in need. So he went and hired himself out to a citizen of that land, who sent him out to his fields to feed pigs. And he was longing to feed himself with the pods that the pigs were eating; yet no-one gave him anything. Then he came to his senses and thought, 'How many of my father's employees have an abundance of food, and yet here am I dying of hunger! I'll get up and go to my father and say to him, "I have sinned toward God and before you. I am no longer worthy to be called your son. Make me like one of your employees."' So he got up and went to his father.

"He was still some distance away when his father caught sight of him. The father was deeply moved, and running to his son he embraced him and kissed him. The son said, 'Father, I have sinned toward God and before you. I am no longer worthy to be called your son.'

"But the father said to his servants, 'Quick, bring out the best robe and dress him in it; put a ring on his finger and shoes on his feet. Bring the fattened calf and kill it. Let's eat and celebrate, because this son of mine was dead but now is alive again; he was lost but now is found.' And they began to celebrate.

"Now the elder son had been in the field, and as he drew near the house he heard music and dancing. And calling one of the hired hands, he asked what this was all about. He replied, 'Your brother has come and your father has killed the fattened calf, because he has got him back safe and well'.

"The elder son became furious and refused even to enter the house. But his father went outside and pleaded with him. He answered his father, 'Look! I have been slaving for you for so many years, and I have never disobeyed your command. Yet you have never given me even a goat so that I could have a celebration with my friends. But when this son of yours, who has squandered your estate on prostitutes, comes home, you kill the fattened calf for him!'

"But his father said to him, 'My child, you are always with me, and everything that is mine is yours. But we must celebrate and rejoice, because this brother of yours was dead but now is alive, and was lost but now is found.'"

CHAPTER 16

Jesus also said to the disciples, "There was a certain rich man who had a manager. This manager was accused of wasting his master's resources, and so the rich man called him in and said, 'What is this that I hear about you? Give me back your management accounts, for you cannot be my manager any longer.'

"The manager said to himself, 'What am I going to do, for my master is about to take my job away from me? I am not strong enough to dig, and I am ashamed to beg. Ah, I know what I will do, so that when I have been removed from being manager, people will welcome me into their homes.'

"And he called in each of his master's debtors, one at a time. He said to the first, 'How much do you owe my master?' He replied, 'A hundred containers of oil'. So the manager said to him, 'Take your bill, sit down quickly and make it fifty'.

"Then he said to another, 'How much do you owe?' And he replied, 'A hundred measures of wheat'. He said to him, 'Take your bill and make it eighty'.

"Now the master commended the unrighteous manager because he had acted cleverly, because the sons of this age are more cunning than the sons of light when it comes to dealing with their own kind. And so I tell you, make friends for yourselves with unrighteous wealth so that when it fails, they will welcome you into eternal dwellings.

"The one who is faithful with very little will also be faithful with much; and the one who is unrighteous with very little will also be unrighteous with much. If then you have not been faithful with unrighteous wealth, who will entrust you with true riches? And if you have not been faithful with what belongs to someone else, who will give you things of your own? No servant can serve two masters. For he will hate one and love the other; or he will cling to one and despise the other. You cannot serve God and Wealth."[a]

The Pharisees (who loved money) were listening to all this, and mocking him.

So Jesus said to them, "You are the kind of people who justify yourselves before others, but God knows your hearts; for things that people value highly are detestable in God's sight. The Law and the Prophets[b] were in place until John came. Since that

---

a Traditionally 'Mammon'. 'Mammon' means more than simply money; it is the power and attractiveness of wealth and possessions.

b A Jewish way of referring to what we now call the Old Testament; likewise 'Moses and the Prophets' below.

time, the kingdom of God is being announced and everyone is being forcefully urged into it; but it would be easier for heaven and earth to pass away than for the smallest stroke of the law to fall. Everyone who divorces his wife and marries another commits adultery; and a man that marries a divorced woman also commits adultery.

"There was a certain rich man who used to wear the finest clothes and hold magnificent parties every day. A poor man named Lazarus, who was covered in sores, lay ill at his front gate. And Lazarus longed to satisfy his hunger from the scraps that fell from the rich man's table. What is more, the dogs used to come and lick his sores.

"Now eventually Lazarus died and was carried by the angels to the side of Abraham.[c] The rich man also died and was buried. And being in the place of the dead and in torment, he looked up and saw Abraham at a great distance, with Lazarus by his side.

"He cried out, 'Father Abraham, be merciful to me! Send Lazarus to dip the tip of his finger in some water to cool my tongue, for I am in agony in this fire.'

"But Abraham replied, 'My child, remember that you received your good things in your lifetime, and in the same way Lazarus received bad things. Now he is comforted here, but you are in agony. And in any case, between us and you a great chasm has been established, so that those who want to go over from here to you are not able to; nor is it possible to cross over from there to us.'

"He replied, 'Then, I beg you, Father, to send Lazarus to my father's house, for I have five brothers. He could warn them so that they might not also come to this place of torment.'

"But Abraham replied, 'They have Moses and the Prophets. Let your brothers listen to them.'

"But the rich man said, 'No, Father Abraham! But if someone were to go to them from the dead, they would repent.'

"He replied, 'If they do not listen to Moses and the Prophets, they will not be persuaded even if someone rises from the dead.'"

c A way of saying that he was brought into God's presence (or heaven).

CHAPTER 17

Jesus said to his disciples, "It is inevitable that stumbling blocks should come, but woe to the person through whom they come. It would be better for him to have a mill-stone tied round his neck and be thrown into the sea than to cause one of these little ones to stumble. Watch yourselves closely. If your brother sins, rebuke him; and if he repents, forgive him. Even if he sins against you seven times in a single day, and seven times turns back to you and says, 'I repent', then you must forgive him."

And the apostles said to the Lord, "Increase our faith!"

But the Lord said, "If you have faith even as small as a mustard seed, you can say to a mulberry tree, 'Be uprooted and planted in the sea', and it will obey you.

"Imagine you have a servant to plough the field or look after the sheep. When he comes in from the field, which of you would say to him, 'Come at once, and recline at the table'? No, you would say to him, 'Prepare my dinner and dress yourself to wait on me while I dine, and afterwards you may eat and drink'. Do you thank the servant for doing what he was commanded to do? It is the same with you. When you have done everything you have been commanded, you should say, 'We are unworthy servants; we have only done what we were supposed to'."

On the way to Jerusalem, Jesus was passing through the border region between Samaria and Galilee. As he entered one particular town, they met ten lepers, standing at a distance. The lepers called out, "Jesus, Master, be merciful to us!"

And when Jesus saw them, he replied, "Go and show yourselves to the priests". And while they were going, they were made whole.

When one of them realised that he had been healed, he came back, honouring and praising God in a loud voice. He fell on his face at Jesus' feet and thanked him. And he was a Samaritan.

Jesus responded, "Weren't there ten who were made clean? Where are the other nine? Did none come back to give honour and praise to God except this foreigner?" And he said to him, "Stand up, and go on your way. Your faith has rescued you."

Once, when he had been asked by the Pharisees when the

kingdom of God was coming, he replied, "The coming of the kingdom of God is something that cannot be closely observed; nor will they say, 'Look, it is here, or there'. For the kingdom of God is in the midst of you."

He said to the disciples, "Days are coming when you will long to see one of the days of the Son of Man, and you will not see it. And they will say, 'Look, it is there! Look, it is here!' Do not go; and do not follow them. For the Son of Man in his day will be like flashes of lightning that light up the sky from one horizon to the other. But first he must suffer many things and be rejected by this generation. In the days of the Son of Man, it will be just as it was in the days of Noah—they were eating, drinking, marrying and giving in marriage, until the day Noah entered the ark, and the flood came and destroyed them all. A similar thing happened in the days of Lot—people were eating, drinking, buying, selling, planting and building. But on the day Lot left Sodom, fire and sulphur rained from heaven and destroyed them all. It will be just the same on the day when the Son of Man is revealed. On that day, no-one who is on the roof should go down into his house to get his belongings; and likewise, no-one who is in the field should turn back. Remember Lot's wife. Whoever tries to preserve his life will lose it; but whoever loses it will keep it alive.

"I say to you, on that night, two men will be reclining on one couch at the table—one will be taken and the other left. Two women will be grinding grain together—one will be taken but the other left."[a]

They answered him, "Where, Lord?" And he said to them, "Where the body is, there the vultures gather".

CHAPTER 18

Then Jesus told them a parable to the effect that they should always pray and not be discouraged. He said, "In a certain city there was a judge who had no fear of God and no respect for other people. And there was a widow in that city, who often would come

a Some ancient manuscripts add: "Two men will be in a field—one will be taken but the other left."

to him, saying, 'Please give me justice over my opponent'.

"For some time he was not willing to help. But later he said to himself, 'Though I have no fear of God and no respect for other people, yet because this widow keeps troubling me I will help her get justice. Otherwise, she will eventually wear me out by her constant approaches.'"

Then the Lord said, "Listen to what the unjust judge says. Will not God, then, bring justice for his chosen people, who cry out to him day and night? Does he delay in helping them? I tell you, he will bring justice for them quickly. However, when the Son of Man comes, will he find such faithfulness in the land?"

He also told this parable to some who were convinced of their own righteousness and had contempt for the rest: "Two men went up to the temple to pray. One was a Pharisee, the other a tax collector. The Pharisee stood and prayed about himself, 'God, I thank you that I am not like the rest of humanity: swindlers, unrighteous, adulterers, or even like this tax collector. I fast two days a week; I give away a tenth of everything I earn.'

"But the tax collector stood at a distance and would not look up to heaven. Instead, he beat his chest and said, 'God, please be merciful to me, the sinner!'

"I tell you, this man was the one that God considered righteous, not the other one. For everyone who lifts himself up will be humbled, but everyone who humbles himself will be exalted."

People were bringing infants to Jesus so that he might touch them. When they saw this, the disciples rebuked them. But Jesus summoned them and said, "Allow the children to come to me; do not prevent them. For the kingdom of God is for ones like these. Truly, I tell you, whoever does not accept the kingdom of God like a child will not enter it."

A certain leader asked him, "Good teacher, what should I do to inherit eternal life?"

Jesus said to him, "Why do you speak of me as 'good'? No-one is good except God alone. You know the commandments: do not commit adultery; do not murder; do not steal; do not give false evidence; honour your father and mother."

He replied, "I have kept all these things since my youth".

When Jesus heard this, he said to him, "You still lack one thing. Sell everything you have and give the proceeds to the poor, and you will have a treasure in heaven. And come follow me!" But when the man heard this he became very sad, for he was very rich.

Jesus looked at him and said, "How difficult it is for those who have wealth to enter into the kingdom of God. Indeed, it is easier for a camel to enter through the eye of a needle than for a rich person to enter the kingdom of God."

Those hearing this said, "Then who is able to be rescued?"

Jesus replied, "What is humanly impossible is possible for God".

Then Peter said, "Look, we have left our homes and followed you".

And Jesus replied, "Truly, I tell you, there is no-one who has left house or wife or brothers or parents or children for the sake of the kingdom of God who will not receive much more in this present age, and in the age to come eternal life".

Then he took the twelve aside and said to them, "Look, we are going up to Jerusalem, and everything written by the prophets about the Son of Man will be accomplished. For he will be handed over to people from other nations, and be ridiculed and insulted and spat upon. They will flog him, then kill him, and on the third day he will be raised to life." Yet they did not grasp any of these things; this saying remained hidden from them and they did not understand what was said.

As Jesus approached Jericho, a certain blind man was sitting beside the road begging. When he heard the crowd going by, he asked what was happening. They explained to him that Jesus from Nazareth was passing by. Then he shouted out, "Jesus, son of David, be merciful to me".

Those in the front of the crowd rebuked him, insisting that he be quiet. But he cried out all the more, "Son of David, be merciful to me".

Jesus stopped and ordered the man to be brought to him. As the man approached, Jesus asked him, "What do you want me to do for you?"

"Lord", he replied, "I want to see again".

Jesus said to him, "Then see again! Your faith has saved[a] you."

Immediately, he was able to see again. And he followed after Jesus, honouring and praising God. When all the people saw this, they gave praise to God.

CHAPTER 19

Jesus entered Jericho and was passing through it. There was a man there named Zacchaeus, a senior tax collector, who was rich. He was trying to see who Jesus was, but he was unable to, because he was a small man and the crowd got in the way. He ran ahead of the crowd, and climbed up a fig tree to see him, because Jesus was about to pass by that way.

When Jesus got to that place, he looked up and said to him, "Zacchaeus, climb down now, because I have to stay in your home today". He climbed down quickly and welcomed Jesus gladly into his home.

When everyone saw this, they complained, "He has gone to stay with a man who is a sinner".

But Zacchaeus stood up and said to the Lord, "Look, half of my belongings, Lord, I will give away to the poor. And if I have cheated anyone out of anything, I will repay them four times the amount."

Then Jesus said to him, "Today salvation has come to this home, for this man too is a son of Abraham. For the Son of Man came to seek out and save what was lost."

While they were still listening, Jesus went on to tell them a parable, because he was close to Jerusalem and the people were thinking that the kingdom of God was just about to appear. He said, "A certain nobleman went to a distant land to receive kingly authority and then return. He called ten of his servants, gave them ten minas[b] and said to them, 'Do business with these while I am gone'.

a Or 'healed', or 'rescued', or 'delivered'.
b A mina was about three months' wages for a labourer.

"However, his citizens hated him and sent a delegation after him, saying, 'We do not want this man to reign over us'. Yet he did receive his kingly authority, and when he returned he had those servants to whom he had given money summoned before him, so that he could find out what profit they had made in business.

"The first one came and said, 'Lord, your single mina has earned ten minas'. He said to him, 'Well done, good servant. Because you have been faithful with a small thing, take authority over ten of my cities.'

"The second came saying, 'Lord, your single mina has made five minas'. And to this one also he said, 'Take authority over five of my cities'.

"Another one came saying, 'Look, Lord, here is the single mina, which I kept stored away in a handkerchief. I was afraid of you, because you are a strict man, taking what you did not deposit and reaping what you did not sow.'

"He replied, 'You wicked servant! By the words of your own mouth I will judge you. You knew, did you, that I was a strict man, taking what I did not deposit and reaping what I did not sow? Why then did you not give my money to a bank? At least then, on my return, I could have collected it with some interest.' And he said to those present, 'Take the mina from him and give it to the one who has ten minas'.

"They replied to him, 'Lord, he already has ten minas!'

"And he said, 'I tell you, everyone who has something will be given more; but from the one who has nothing, even what he has will be taken away. But as for those enemies of mine who did not want me to reign over them, bring them here and execute them before me.'"

After saying these things, Jesus kept moving on up to Jerusalem.

As Jesus neared Bethphage and Bethany, at the place called the Mount of Olives, he sent out two of the disciples, saying, "Go into the town opposite. As you enter, you will find a colt tied up there on which no-one has ever ridden. Untie it and bring it here. If someone asks you, 'Why are you untying the colt?' say

'Because the Lord needs it'."

Those who had been sent went off and found things just as Jesus had told them. As they were untying the colt, its owners said to them, "Why are you untying the colt?" And they said, "Because the Lord needs it".

They brought the colt to Jesus, threw their cloaks over it and got Jesus to sit on it. As he rode along, others spread out their cloaks on the road. Now as he neared the place where the road descends the Mount of Olives, the whole crowd of disciples began to praise God joyfully and loudly because of all the mighty deeds they had seen. They declared, "Blessed be the king who comes in the name of the Lord! Peace in heaven and glory in the highest."

Yet some of the Pharisees in the crowd called out to Jesus, "Teacher, rebuke your disciples!"

Jesus replied, "I tell you, if they were to keep quiet, the stones would cry out".

As Jesus came near and saw the city, he wept over it. He said, "How I wish that you—of all places—had recognised this day the things that bring peace! But now they are hidden from your eyes. For days are coming upon you when your enemies will set up a barricade against your walls. They will surround you and trap you from every side. They will destroy you and your children within your walls, and they will not leave one single stone upon another within you. And all this because you did not recognise the time of your visitation."

Then he entered the temple court and began to drive out those who were selling things there. He said to them, "In the Scriptures it is written, 'My house will be a house of prayer', but you have made it into a hideout for robbers!"

He was teaching daily in the temple court. But the chief priests, scribes and leaders of the people were trying to kill him. Yet they could not find a way to do it, because all the people were hanging on his every word.

CHAPTER 20

One day, as he was teaching the people in the temple court and announcing the great news, the chief priests and the scribes approached him together with the elders. They said to him, "Tell us, by what authority are you doing these things? Or who is the one who gives you this authority?"

He answered, "I will also ask you something; now you tell me: was the baptism of John from heaven or of human origin?"

They debated this among themselves, saying, "If we say, 'From heaven', he will say, 'Then why didn't you believe in him?' But if we say, 'Of human origin', all the people will stone us because they are convinced that John was a prophet." And so they answered that they did not know where it was from.

Jesus said to them, "Nor will I tell you by what authority I am doing these things".

He began to tell the people this parable: "A man planted a vineyard and leased it to some farmers, and went away for quite some time. After a while, he sent a servant to the farmers so that they might give him his share of the vineyard's produce. But the farmers beat the servant and sent him away with nothing. Then he sent another servant, but they beat him also, treated him shamefully and sent him away with nothing. Then he sent a third one, but they hurt him also, and threw him out.

"Now the master of the vineyard said, 'What will I do? I will send my beloved son; perhaps they will respect him.'

"But when the farmers saw him they reasoned with one another, 'This is the heir. Let's kill him so that the inheritance will be ours.' So they threw him out of the vineyard and killed him.

"So then, what will the master of the vineyard do to them? He will come and destroy those farmers, and give the vineyard to others."

When those who were listening heard this, they exclaimed, "May it never be!"

But Jesus looked straight at them and said, "What then is the meaning of this passage of Scripture: 'The stone that the builders rejected has become the cornerstone'? Everyone who falls upon that stone will be broken to pieces, and anyone on whom it falls will be crushed."

The scribes and chief priests wanted to lay their hands on him at that very moment because they knew he had told this parable against them; but they were afraid of the people.

So they kept a close eye on him by sending spies who pretended to be sincere. They wanted to trap him in something he said, so that they could hand him over to the rule and authority of the Roman Governor. They asked him, "Teacher, we know that you speak and teach correctly; that you do not show favouritism, but instead teach the way of God truthfully. Is it lawful for us Jews to pay a tax to Caesar, or not?"

Jesus saw through their trickery and said to them, "Show me a silver coin: whose image and inscription is on it?"

"Caesar's", they said.

He responded, "Well then, repay to Caesar the things that are Caesar's, and to God the things that are God's". They were not able to catch him out in his words in front of the people. They were amazed at his answer and became silent.

Some men from the faction of the Sadducees[a]—who say there is no resurrection—came to him. They asked him, "Teacher, Moses wrote for us that if a man's brother dies having a wife but no children, the man should marry his dead brother's wife and raise up children for his brother. Now suppose there were seven brothers. The first brother married and died without children. The second brother married her, then the third, and so on, until all seven brothers had died and left no children. Later, the woman herself died. In the time of resurrection, therefore, whose wife will the woman be, since all seven men had married her?"

Jesus said to them, "The people of this age marry and are given in marriage, but those who are counted worthy of sharing in that age and in the resurrection from the dead will not marry or be given in marriage, for they can no longer die—they will be like angels. They will be God's children since they are children of the resurrection. Moses also revealed that the dead rise, in the

a The Sadducees were a fairly secular group within Judaism, mainly from the ruling class.

passage about the burning bush,[b] where he called the Lord 'the God of Abraham, and the God of Isaac, and the God of Jacob'. Now God is not the God of the dead but of the living, for they are all alive in him."

Some of the scribes responded, "Teacher, you have spoken well". For they no longer dared to put any questions to him.

Then Jesus said to them, "How is it that they say the Christ is to be the son of David? After all, in the book of Psalms, David himself says, 'The Lord said to my lord, "Sit at my right hand until I make your enemies a footstool for your feet"'. David therefore calls the Christ 'Lord'; so how can he also be David's son?"

In the hearing of all the people, Jesus said to the disciples, "Beware of the scribes, who like to walk about in long robes, and love to be greeted by people in the markets and to have the best seats in the synagogues and the places of honour at banquets. They devour the homes of widows and pretentiously say long public prayers. They will receive more severe judgement."

CHAPTER 21

Jesus looked up and noticed the rich dropping their gifts into the temple treasury. And he saw a poor widow drop in two small copper coins. He said, "Truly, I tell you that this poor widow has given more than all of them. For they all gave from their surplus, but she, in her poverty, gave all that she had to live on."

When some were speaking about how the temple had been adorned with beautiful stones and offerings, he said, "These stones you are looking at—days are coming when not one stone will be left on another; they will all be torn down".

And they asked him, "Teacher, when will these things be, and what will be the sign that they are about to happen?"

He replied, "See that you are not deceived, for many will come in my name saying, 'I am he' and 'The time is near'. Do not go after them. When you hear of wars and rebellions, do not

b Jesus is referring to Exodus chapter 3, in the Old Testament, where God appears to Moses in a burning bush.

panic. For these things must happen first, but the end will not follow at once."

Then he said to them, "Nation will rise against nation, and kingdom against kingdom. There will be great earthquakes, and famines and plagues in various places, and terrors and great signs in the sky. But before all these things, they will seize you and persecute you, handing you over to the synagogues and prisons, and bringing you before kings and governors for the sake of my name. This will be your opportunity to bear witness. Make up your mind, then, not to prepare your defence beforehand; for I will give you words and wisdom that none of your opponents will be able to withstand or contradict. You will be betrayed by parents and brothers and relatives and friends. They will put some of you to death, and you will be hated by all sorts of people because of my name. Yet not a hair of your head will be lost. Through your endurance, you will gain your lives.

"But when you see Jerusalem surrounded by armies, then know that her ruin is close. At that time, those in Judea must flee to the hills, and those in the city itself must get out, and those in the country must not enter it. For these will be days when justice is dealt out, so that all that is written in the Scriptures might be fulfilled. Woe to those who are pregnant and to nursing mothers in those days, for there will be great distress in the land and wrath[a] upon this people; and they will fall by the edge of the sword and be carried off captive to all the other nations, and Jerusalem will be trampled by the nations, until the times of the nations are fulfilled.

"There will be signs in the sun and moon and stars. On the earth there will be great anxiety among the nations, as they become confused at the roaring and fury of the sea. People will faint from fear and foreboding of what is coming on the world; for the powers of heaven will be shaken. And then you will see the Son of Man coming in a cloud with power and great glory. When these things start to happen, stand up and lift your heads, for your redemption is near."

a   That is, anger, judgement, divine retribution.

And he told them a parable: "Look at the fig tree, and all the trees. When they sprout leaves, you can see and know for yourselves that summer is near. In the same way, when you see these things happening, know that the kingdom of God is near. Truly, I tell you that this generation will not pass away until everything has taken place. Heaven and earth will pass away, but my words will not pass away.

"Watch yourselves, so that your hearts will not be weighed down by decadence, drunkenness, and the anxieties of everyday life, and that day come upon you suddenly like a trap. For it will come upon all those who live on the face of the earth. But watch at all times, praying that you will have the strength to escape these things that are about to take place, and stand before the Son of Man."

By day, Jesus was teaching in the temple court, but at night he went out and stayed on the Mount of Olives. And all the people would rise early in the morning and come to the temple to listen to him.

CHAPTER 22

Now the festival of the Unleavened Bread, which is known as the Passover,[a] was approaching, and the chief priests and the scribes were searching for how they might do away with Jesus, for they were frightened of the people. Then Satan entered Judas (who was called Iscariot and who was one of the twelve). He went and spoke with the chief priests and the temple guards about how he could betray Jesus to them. They were delighted, and arranged to give him money. He agreed, and so began to look for an opportunity to hand Jesus over to them without a crowd present.

Now the day of Unleavened Bread arrived, on which the Passover lamb had to be sacrificed. So Jesus sent Peter and John out, saying, "Go and prepare the Passover meal for us so that we may eat it".

a One of the great festivals of the Jewish year, on which the Jews remember and celebrate their escape (or Exodus) from slavery in Egypt.

"Where would you like us to prepare it?" they said.

He replied, "As you enter the city, a man carrying a jar of water will meet you. Follow him to the house he goes into, and say to the owner of the house, 'The teacher asks you, "Where is the room in which I may eat the Passover meal with my disciples?"' And he will show you a large furnished room upstairs. Prepare things there."

So they went and found things just the way he had said, and they made preparations for the Passover meal.

When the time came, Jesus reclined at the table with his apostles. He said to them, "I have longed to eat this Passover meal with you before I suffer. For I tell you, I will not eat it again until it has reached its fulfilment in the kingdom of God."

He took a cup of wine, gave thanks for it and said, "Take this and share it among yourselves. For I tell you, from now on I will not drink of the fruit of the vine until the kingdom of God comes."

He took a loaf of bread, gave thanks for it, broke it and gave it to them, saying, "This is my body which is given for you; do this in remembrance of me".

And in the same way, after eating the meal, he took the cup of wine and said, "This cup is the new covenant in my blood, which is poured out for you. But see, the hand of my betrayer is with me on the table. For the Son of Man is going just as it has been determined. Yet woe to that man by whom he is betrayed." Then they began to discuss among themselves which one of them was about to do this.

An argument arose among them as to which of them might be regarded as the greatest. So he said to them, "The kings of the other nations dominate their subjects, and those placed in authority over the subjects are called 'benefactors'. But it is not to be so with you. Rather, the greatest among you is to become like the youngest, and the one who leads like the one who serves. For who is greater—the one who reclines at the table or the one serving the meal? It is the one who reclines at the table, is it not? Yet I myself am among you as one who serves.

"You are the ones who have stood by me during my hardships.

And just as my Father gave me kingly authority, I give the same to you, so that you may eat and drink at my table in my kingdom. And you will sit upon thrones judging the twelve tribes of Israel.

"Simon, Simon, listen! Satan has insisted that he sift you all like wheat, but I have prayed for you, Peter, that your faith might not fail. And when you have turned back, strengthen your brothers."

Peter said to Jesus, "Lord, I am prepared to go with you to prison and to death!"

But Jesus replied, "I tell you, Peter, before the rooster crows today, you will have denied knowing me three times". Then he said to them, "When I sent you out without a wallet, bag or sandals, did you lack anything?"

"Nothing", they answered.

He said to them, "Now, however, whoever has a wallet, take it; likewise, a bag. Whoever does not have a sword should sell his cloak and buy one. For I tell you, this piece of Scripture must be fulfilled in my life: 'He was considered as one of the outlaws'. Indeed, even now it is being fulfilled."

Then they said, "Look, Lord, here are two swords!"

"That is enough", he replied.

Then Jesus left the house and made his way to the Mount of Olives, where he usually went, and the disciples followed him. When they reached the place, he said to them, "Pray that you will not enter into temptation". And he withdrew about a stone's throw from them, knelt down and prayed: "Father, if you are willing, please take this cup[b] away from me. Nevertheless, may your will be done, not mine."[c]

And rising up from his prayer, he returned to his disciples and found them asleep because of their grief. He asked them, "Why do you sleep? Get up, and pray that you will not enter into temptation."

b 'Drinking the cup' is an Old Testament way of talking about receiving punishment or judgement, a bit like the English expression 'taking your medicine'.
c Some ancient manuscripts add: "An angel from heaven appeared to him, and strengthened him. And being in great distress, he prayed all the more earnestly, and his sweat was like drops of blood falling to the ground."

While he was still speaking, a mob appeared and the man named Judas, one of the twelve, was leading them. He approached Jesus to kiss him, but Jesus said, "Judas, are you betraying the Son of Man with a kiss?"

Seeing what was about to happen, those around him said, "Lord, should we strike with the sword?" And one of them struck the chief priest's servant and cut off his right ear.

But Jesus answered them, "Enough of this". And he touched his ear and healed him.

Jesus said to those who had come to arrest him, the chief priests and captains of the temple guard and elders, "Have you come with swords and clubs, as if I am a criminal? I was with you daily in the temple, and you did not lay a hand on me. But this is your hour; this is the authority of darkness."

Then they seized him and led him away, and took him to the chief priest's house. Peter followed at a distance. A fire had been lit in the middle of the courtyard, and Peter sat down with those who were around it. A servant girl noticed him sitting in the light, and she stared at him, and said, "This one also was with him".

But Peter denied it: "Woman, I do not know him".

A short time later, someone else looked at him and said, "You are one of them as well".

But Peter said, "Sir, I am not".

An hour or so later, another one said quite emphatically, "Certainly, this man was also with him; in fact, he is a Galilean".

But Peter said, "Sir, I do not know what you are talking about". And immediately, while he was still speaking, the rooster crowed. The Lord turned and looked at Peter, and Peter remembered the Lord's prediction, how he had said to him, 'Before the rooster crows today, you will deny me three times'. And Peter went outside and wept bitterly.

Now the men who were guarding Jesus mocked him and beat him. They blindfolded him and asked him, "Prophesy! Who is it who struck you?" And they heaped many other insults on him.

As day broke, the elders of the people, the chief priests and the scribes gathered together, and Jesus was led out before their Council.

They inquired, "If you are the Christ, tell us so!"

But he replied, "If I were to tell you, you would not believe. And if I were to ask you a question, you would not answer. But from this time on, the Son of Man will be seated at God's right hand of power."

They all said, "So you are the Son of God?"

But he replied, "You say that I am".

And they responded, "What more testimony do we need? We have heard it from his own mouth."

CHAPTER 23

Then the whole Council rose and brought him to Governor Pilate. They began to accuse him, saying, "We found this man perverting our nation and forbidding people to pay taxes to Caesar, and saying that he himself is Christ, a king".

So Pilate asked him, "Are you the King of the Jews?"

Jesus answered, "You say so".

Pilate said to the chief priests and the crowds, "I can find no fault with this man".

But they grew more insistent: "He is stirring up the people, teaching throughout the whole of Judea, starting in Galilee and ending up here".

When Pilate heard this, he asked whether the man was from Galilee. And when he discovered that Jesus was under Herod's jurisdiction, he sent him to Herod, who was himself in Jerusalem at that time.

Now when Herod saw Jesus he was overjoyed. He had been wanting to see Jesus for some time, because he had heard about him, and hoped to see him perform some miraculous sign. He questioned him at length, but Jesus said nothing in reply.

The chief priests and the scribes stood there, vehemently accusing him. And Herod held Jesus in contempt. With the help of his soldiers, he ridiculed him, dressed him in shining clothes, and sent him back to Pilate. (On that day, Herod and Pilate became friends with each other; for previously there had been hostility between them.)

Pilate called together the chief priests, the leaders and the people, and said to them, "You brought this man to me as one who was perverting the people. I interrogated him in your presence, but found no basis for any of your accusations against him. Moreover, neither did Herod, for he sent him back to us. It seems obvious that he has done nothing deserving of death. Therefore, I will order a flogging, and then release him."[a]

But they cried out together, "Take him away! Release Barabbas to us!" (Barabbas was in prison for a rebellion that had occurred in the city, and for murder.)

Pilate wanted to release Jesus, and so he spoke to them again. But they cried out, "Crucify! Crucify him!"

A third time, Pilate said to them, "For what? Has he done anything evil? I have found that this man committed no crime deserving of death. Therefore, I will order a flogging, and then release him."

But the crowd kept demanding with loud voices that he be crucified; and their voices won out. Pilate decided to grant their request. He released the man who had been imprisoned for rebellion and murder—as they requested—and gave Jesus up to what they wanted.

And as they led him away, they seized a man named Simon (from Cyrene) who was coming in from the country. They laid the cross on him, and made him carry it behind Jesus.

Now a great crowd of people followed him, including women who were mourning and wailing for him. Jesus turned to them and said, "Daughters of Jerusalem, do not weep over me; but weep for yourselves and for your children. For days are coming when they will say, 'Blessed are the barren women, and the wombs that have borne no children, and the breasts that have never nursed'. At that time, they will say to the mountains, 'Fall on us' and to the hills, 'Cover us'. For if this is what they do when the tree is green, what will happen when it is withered?"

Two others who were criminals were also led out with him to

a Some ancient manuscripts add: "On account of the festival, he was obliged to release one man to them."

be executed. And when they arrived at the place called 'The Skull', they crucified him there along with the criminals—one on Jesus' right, the other on his left.[b] And the soldiers divided his clothing by placing bets; and the people stood by, watching.

The leaders even made fun of him, saying, "He rescued others; let him rescue himself if he really is God's Christ, his Chosen One".

The soldiers also ridiculed him, coming up and offering him bitter wine. They said, "If you really are the King of the Jews, rescue yourself". There was a placard above him which read: THIS IS THE KING OF THE JEWS.

One of the criminals who hung there was abusing Jesus, saying, "Aren't you supposed to be the Christ? Rescue yourself and us!"

But the other criminal responded with a rebuke: "Have you no fear of God? After all, you are under the same death sentence. Yet, we are here justly; we are receiving what we deserve for our actions, but he has done nothing wrong."

Then he said, "Jesus, please remember me when you come into your kingdom".

And Jesus replied, "I tell you the truth, today you will be with me in Paradise".

By this time, it was already about midday, but darkness came over the whole land until three in the afternoon, because the sun stopped shining. The curtain of the temple was torn down the middle. Then Jesus cried out in a loud voice, "Father, into your hands I entrust my spirit!" With these words he breathed his last breath.

When the centurion saw what happened, he honoured and praised God, saying, "This man was truly the Righteous One". When the crowd that had gathered for this spectacle saw these things, they beat their chests and returned to their homes. But all Jesus' acquaintances and the women who had followed him from Galilee stood at a distance, watching these things.

Now there was a man named Joseph, who was a member of the Council. He was a good and just man, and had not given his

b Some ancient manuscripts add: "And Jesus said, 'Father, forgive them, for they do not know what they are doing'."

consent to their decision and action. He came from the Jewish town of Arimathea and was waiting expectantly for the kingdom of God. He approached Pilate and asked for the body of Jesus. And when he had taken it down from the cross, he wrapped it in linen and placed it in a tomb cut out from rock in which no-one had ever been laid.

It was the Day of Preparation, and the Sabbath was drawing near, but still the women who had accompanied Jesus from Galilee followed Joseph and took note of the tomb and how Jesus' body was laid there. Returning home, they prepared some burial perfumes and lotions. But on the Sabbath Day they rested according to the commandment.

CHAPTER 24

Very early on Sunday morning, the women went to the tomb carrying the burial lotions they had prepared. They found the stone door rolled away from the tomb, but when they went in they did not find the body of the Lord Jesus. And as they stood there perplexed about this, suddenly two men in gleaming clothes approached them.

The women were terrified, and bowed down with their faces to the ground. The men said to them, "Why do you search for the living among the dead? He is not here; he has been raised! Remember how he told you while he was still in Galilee, 'The Son of Man must be betrayed into the hands of sinful people and be crucified, and on the third day be raised up'."

The women remembered Jesus' words, and returning from the tomb, they told all these things to the eleven apostles and all the other people there. (The women were Mary Magdalene, Joanna, Mary the mother of James, and some others with them.) Yet the apostles did not believe them, because these reports seemed like nonsense to them.

All the same, Peter got up and ran to the tomb. Bending over, he saw the burial clothes lying by themselves. He returned home, wondering at what had happened.

Now that same day, two of them were travelling to a town about eleven kilometres[a] from Jerusalem, called Emmaus. They were talking with each other about all that had happened. And while they were talking and discussing, Jesus himself approached them and began to walk alongside them. But their eyes were kept from recognising him.

He asked them, "What are these things you are discussing with each other as you walk along?"

They stood there looking sad, and one of them, named Cleopas, asked, "Are you the only visitor to Jerusalem who does not know about the events that have taken place there in these days?"

"What events?" he asked.

They replied, "The events surrounding Jesus of Nazareth, who was a prophet powerful in word and deed before God and all the people, and how the chief priests and our leaders handed him over to death and crucified him. We were hoping that he was the one who was going to redeem Israel. But besides all of this, it is now the third day since all these things happened. And then to add to it, some women from our group astonished us. They were at the tomb early this morning, and when they didn't find the body they came saying that they had seen a vision of angels, who said he was alive. And some of those with us went back to the tomb and found it exactly as the women described, but they did not see him."

And Jesus said to them, "How foolish you are, and slow of heart to believe all the things the prophets foretold! Didn't the Christ have to suffer these things and so enter his glory?" And beginning with the writings of Moses and all the prophets, he explained to them the things written about himself in all the Scriptures.

They approached the town where they were going and Jesus gave the impression he was going further on. But they urged him, "Stay with us, because it is evening; the day is already over".

So he went in to stay with them. When he was reclining at the table with them, he took the loaf of bread, gave thanks, broke it and gave it to them. Then their eyes were opened and they

a Literally, 'sixty stadia'.

recognised him, but he disappeared from their sight. They said to one another, "Were not our hearts on fire as he spoke to us on the road and explained the Scriptures to us?"

They got up straight away and returned to Jerusalem, where they found the eleven apostles and those with them gathered together, who said, "The Lord really has been raised to life, and he has appeared to Simon". Then the two related the things that had happened on the road, and how they had recognised him when he broke the loaf of bread.

While they were talking about these things, Jesus stood right in the middle of them and said, "Peace to you". But they were startled and terrified, because they thought they were seeing a ghost.

And Jesus said to them, "Why are you disturbed, and why do doubts arise in your hearts? Look at my hands and feet, for it is really me. Touch me and see, for a ghost does not have flesh and bones, as you can see I have." He said this, and showed them his hands and feet. But when they still did not believe because of joy and amazement, he said to them, "Do you have anything here I can eat?" So they handed him a piece of cooked fish. He took it and ate it right in front of them.

Then he said to them, "I told you about these things while I was still with you: everything that is written about me in the Law of Moses, the Prophets and the Psalms had to be fulfilled". Then he opened their minds to understand the Scriptures and said, "This is what is written: the Christ will suffer and rise from the dead on the third day, and repentance for the forgiveness of sins will be announced in his name to all nations, beginning from Jerusalem.

"You are witnesses of these things, and so I will send to you the promise of my Father. You yourselves stay here in the city until you are clothed with power from on high."

Then he led them out to Bethany. He raised his hands and blessed them, and as he was blessing them, he departed from them and was taken up into heaven. They worshipped him, and then returned to Jerusalem with great joy, where they were always in the temple court, praising God.

Where to from here?

Everybody who met the real Jesus in the flesh had a reaction. You've just met him through the pages of this book. What reaction do you have, and what should you do about it?

It would be a mistake to be like the rich leader in chapter 18, who met Jesus but chose his money (p. 56).

Or to be like the religious Pharisees, who listened to what Jesus had to say but preferred to trust in their own goodness (p. 56).

Much better to be like the runaway younger son in chapter 15, who made some bad choices but decided to come home (p. 50).

Whatever your reaction to Jesus, it would be helpful to talk about it with someone who has been following Jesus for a while. You might like to:

- **Connect** with the person or group who gave you this book.
- **Visit** the website printed on the back cover.
- **Find** a local church that teaches the Bible.

In the next few pages, you'll find a useful summary of the Gospel of Jesus and what it means.

Why Jesus is essential

Luke's Gospel tells us a lot about Jesus—about who he was, and what he said and did. What does it mean for us today?

To answer that, we need to remind ourselves of what happened 'previously in the Bible' (see pages 4-6). Three main points came out of the first half of the Bible:

1. God is the good and loving creator of the world, and therefore the ruler and king of the world. God created humanity too, and put us in charge of the world, but under his authority. This could be illustrated like this, with a crown representing God as king:

2. From the beginning, we rebelled against our creator and ruler, and defied his authority. The very first humans did this, and we have all been doing it ever since. It's as if we step out from under God's rule, and say that we don't want to be part of his kingdom. We declare that we ourselves are in charge, like this:

3. Rebelling against God the King is an act of treason. It's rejecting and defying the good God who made us. And God is too good and too just to let that rebellion continue. One day we will all have to stand before him and be judged for not treating him as God. On that day, the Bible says, God will establish his kingdom once more, and all those who are rebels against him will be shut out of his kingdom, and suffer death and everlasting ruin.

The first half of the Bible ends with tension in the air. God has promised that he will come and re-establish his kingdom,

defeat all his enemies, and save his people. But what if everyone is his enemy and deserving of judgement? What if even his own people Israel have rejected him? What then? Is God going to bring in his kingdom at last only to have no-one in it?

And so we come to Jesus.

4. Jesus the Christ, and God's rescue plan

Right from the beginning of Luke's Gospel, Luke lets us know that Jesus is the coming king or Christ, who will reign over God's new kingdom. Jesus comes telling people what the 'kingdom of God' will be like, and urging them to get ready for it.

But Jesus wasn't the sort of Christ or king that many people were expecting. He didn't go around condemning sinners or avoiding them—just the opposite. All through the Gospel of Luke, Jesus keeps meeting rebellious, sinful, 'lost' people, and saving them—like Zacchaeus, the despised tax collector (in chapter 19, p. 58). Zacchaeus has his life turned around, and Jesus says to him, "Today salvation has come to this home, for this man too is a son of Abraham. For the Son of Man came to seek out and save what was lost."

This is a great summary of Jesus' mission. It was a rescue mission, to turn sinful rebels back to God, so that they could belong to his kingdom and enter it when it arrived.

The climax of this mission was his death. Jesus' death on the cross was the very way he rescued the lost.

When you think about it, Jesus didn't deserve to die. Unlike Adam and Eve, or Israel, or any of us, he didn't rebel against God, or deserve any of God's judgement. But he did die—*in our place*, to take the punishment that we deserve. He took the full force of God's judgement on himself, so that forgiveness and pardon might be available for rebels everywhere. As one of the disciples, Peter, later wrote: "Christ suffered once for sins, the righteous on behalf of the unrighteous, to bring you to God" (1 Peter chapter 3, verse 18).

This was God's rescue plan through Jesus: to save us from the punishment we deserve because of our sin.

5. Jesus is the risen Christ, God's king

Of course Luke's Gospel doesn't end with Jesus' death, but with his resurrection. The resurrection was God's way of saying that Jesus' sacrifice had worked. God raised Jesus up as the king of the coming kingdom.

Two things follow from this. The *first* is that the kingdom really is coming. When it arrives, the risen Lord Jesus Christ will fix up everything that is wrong with this world. He will open the books and call everyone to account for their actions—including you and me. But he will save his own people from that judgement, and they will live with him forever in a new creation: the kingdom of God.

The *second* is that now is the time to get ready for the coming kingdom: to turn back from our rebellion against God, to beg for forgiveness, and to make a fresh start with God. If we stop trying to be the 'king' of our own lives, and allow Jesus to be the rightful

 king, we can be quite sure that when the great day of the kingdom of God comes, we will not fall under the judgement of God for our sins. We will be rescued, and enter his kingdom with joy, because Jesus has died in our place so that all our sins could be forgiven.

6. A choice before us

Jesus presented the people of his day with a choice, and he presents us with the same choice today. We have two options.

Option 1 is to continue in the natural way of all people—that is, to rebel against our creator, and run our lives our own way without him. The end result is that God will give us what we ask for and deserve. When his kingdom comes, he will condemn us for rejecting his rightful rule over our lives, and send us to an eternity of separation from himself, without life or love or relationship.

Option 2 is to realise that our rebellion against God is a lost cause. But if we turn back to God and ask for forgiveness, then everything changes. God accepts Jesus' death as payment in full for our sins, and freely and completely forgives us. He pours his own Spirit into our hearts, and gives us a new life that stretches past death and into eternity. We are no longer rebels, but members of God's own kingdom, with Jesus, God's king, as our ruler.

This is the message and the challenge that Jesus brought not only to Israel, but to the whole world. He brings it to you and me.

Which of the two options sounds like the way you'd like to live?

Next steps

Where you go from here depends on your answer to the challenge of Jesus.

If your answer is that you'd like to live with Jesus as your king, and you know that at present you are not, then the next step is simply to talk to God about it:

- Admit to him that you've rebelled against him.
- Ask for his forgiveness.
- Ask for his help to make a fresh start as a disciple of Jesus.

After that, the best thing to do is to talk to a Christian friend or the person who gave you this book, and find out more about living as a disciple of Jesus. (If you don't know who to contact, go to the website on the back cover of this book.)

If you don't feel ready to make a decision about Jesus, or you still have questions, then the best thing to do is also to talk to someone (a Christian friend, or someone at a local church). Again, if you don't know who to contact, go to the website shown on the back cover of this book for more information.

matthiasmedia

Matthias Media is an independent Christian publishing company with offices in Australia and the US. To browse our online catalogue, download free samples and find out more about our extensive range of books and resources, contact one of our offices or visit one of our websites (listed on page 2).